GW00818454

Richard B. Fisher has a
(with Dr George A. Ch
Health. Both have been p

Dr Fisher has received h
an MSc from Brunel University. After
paperback publisher in the United States and Britain, he
began to write. His next book will be a life of Edward
Jenner. He was born in Cleveland, Ohio, and is now a
British citizen.

RICHARD B. FISHER

A Dictionary of
Body Chemistry

A PALADIN BOOK

GRANADA

London Toronto Sydney New York

Published by Granada Publishing Limited in 1983

ISBN 0 586 08382 0

A Granada Paperback UK Original
Copyright © Richard B. Fisher 1983

Granada Publishing Limited
Frogmore, St Albans, Herts AL2 2NF
and
36 Golden Square, London W1R 4AH
515 Madison Avenue, New York, NY 10022, USA
117 York Street, Sydney, NSW 2000, Australia
100 Skyway Avenue, Rexdale, Ontario, M9W 3A6, Canada
61 Beach Road, Auckland, New Zealand

Printed and bound in Great Britain by
Hazell Watson & Viney Ltd, Aylesbury
Set in Baskerville

Granada ®
Granada Publishing ®

Foreword

Perhaps even more than its predecessors, *A Dictionary of Drugs* and *A Dictionary of Mental Health*, *A Dictionary of Body Chemistry* needs a foreword. In the first place, it makes no pretence to be complete. A glance at the index of any biochemical textbook reveals that there are thousands of chemicals in the body. New ones are discovered frequently, if not daily. The *Dictionary* aims to define those chemicals and their functions in health which people hear or read about in the media or from their doctors. A few omnibus terms like *enzyme*, *hormone*, *transmitter* describe the size and scope of important categories of chemicals.

Because it is written to inform non-specialists, *A Dictionary of Body Chemistry* devotes important entries to *blood*, *body fluid*, *bone* and *lymph*, among others. These are tissues like muscle and skin, not chemicals like *calcium* or *protein*. They consist of living cells, in part at least. Yet calcium is an element – or often, in the body, an *ion* – while the proteins are large, complex and precisely ordered molecules. The blood contains a variable number of elements (or ions) and molecules as well as blood cells. Its familiarity alone justifies its inclusion amongst the chemicals which compose blood.

Unlike *A Dictionary of Drugs*, this volume contains no separate entry on biochemistry and only two general chemical entries, *electrolyte* and ion, both of which are justified because they occur in the body just as do *nucleotides* and *peptides*. Instead, I have added three Appendices:

1. Hydrocarbons and amines
2. pH, equivalents and constants
3. Elements and bonds

Finally, a note of heartfelt thanks: the manuscript was read and criticized by Dr George A Christie, a physician and Managing Director of Grand Metropolitan Biotechnology Ltd, who is the co-author of *A Dictionary of Drugs*. Any errors remaining in the *Dictionary*, however, are entirely my own responsibility.

R.B.F.
London
October 1981

Acetylcholine (ACh)

A *transmitter* of signals between some nerve cells in the brain and spinal cord, between nerve cells and most voluntary muscles, between nerve cells in the parasympathetic nervous system (see *Transmitter*) and some involuntary muscles, and between nerve cells running to the adrenal glands and some other glands. All such nerve cells are *cholinergic*; i.e., energized by acetylocholine.

Acetylcholine is the transmitter synthesized by an important parasympathetic nerve connecting the brain to the heart and gut, the vagus nerve. It is also the transmitter of signals from parasympathetic nerve cells controlling the bladder, uterus and rectum.

The presence of acetylcholine in heart muscle was discovered in 1906, but identification of the role played by the chemical was the work of several scientists beginning with the German biochemist, Otto Loewi, in 1921. The description, cholinergic, was first used by an English physiologist, Sir Henry Hallett Dale. Dale shared the Nobel Prize for medicine and physiology with Loewi in 1936.

Certain muscular diseases not caused by disorders in the brain, for example, myasthenia gravis, are a result of an unexplained failure in the supply of ACh. The treatment of preference is a drug which inhibits the activity of *cholinesterase*, the *enzyme* that breaks down ACh. Diminished supplies of ACh in the brain itself, furthermore, may be a cause of the most common form of dementia, Alzheimer's disease.

ACh is a small molecule with the structural formula:

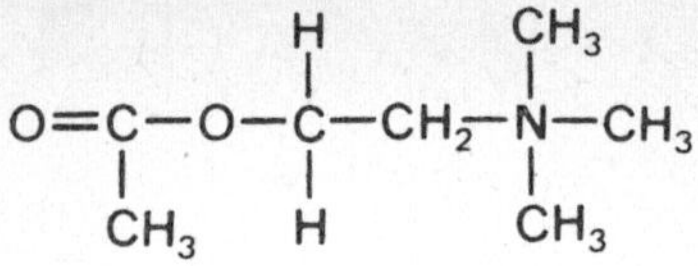

$$O=C-O-\overset{\overset{\displaystyle H}{|}}{C}-CH_2-\overset{\overset{\displaystyle CH_3}{|}}{N}-CH_3$$
$$\overset{|}{CH_3} \quad \overset{|}{H} \quad \overset{|}{CH_3}$$

Acid

(1) (L.: *acidus*, from *acere* = to be sour). Sour. (2) (L.: *acidum*) A chemical compound of an electronegative *ion* (that is, an atom with one or more electrons than protons e.g., *chlorine*) and one or more *hydrogen* ions which may be replaced by an electropositive ion (e.g., sodium). If the electropositive ion is a metal, the new compound is called a *salt*. In water, in the absence of an electropositive ion, an acid will give up hydrogen ions; that is, a proton without an electron. Thus, acids can be defined as substances which lower the pH of a solution (see Appendix 2).

Acids may also be looked upon as the opposite of *bases* in that acids form compounds with bases by accepting electrons from bases, whereas bases form compounds by donating electrons to an acid.

Strong acids such as *hydrochloric acid* tend to give up hydrogen ions readily. They are very corrosive because the electronegative ion binds to any available positive ion. Weak acids taste sour but are much less corrosive. All acids turn litmus paper red.

Important acids in the body include:

Amino acids
Carbonic acid
Citric acid
Deoxyribonucleic acid (DNA)
Folic acid
Gamma-amino butyric acid (GABA)
Hyaluronic acid
Hydrochloric acid
Lactic acid (see *Lactose, Salt*)
Nicotinic acid (see *Niacin*)
Ribonucleic acid (RNA)
Uric acid

ACTH (see *Adrenocorticotropic hormone*)

Actin (see *Myosin*)

Adenine

A base found in *deoxyribonucleic acid* (DNA) and *ribonucleic acid* (RNA), and in the *nucleotides, adenosine triphosphate* and *cyclic adenosine monophosphate*. The complementary base to adenine in the DNA double helix is *thymine*, and in RNA, *uracil*.

Adenine has the structural formula:

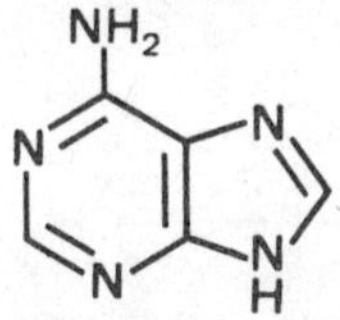

Being a fusion of a pyrimidine (left ring) and an imidazole (right ring), it is one of a class of chemicals called purines. Purines can be synthesized by most cells and may also be obtained from food.

Adenosine triphosphate (ATP)

A nucleotide in which a *base, adenine*, and a *sugar, ribose*, are linked to three phosphate molecules (see *phosphorus*). ATP is of the greatest importance in the body as a storage form of energy to power muscle contraction and a wide range of chemical reactions involved in the synthesis of large molecules such as *enzymes* and nucleic acids (see *deoxyribonucleic acid, ribonucleic acid*). In all such reactions, ATP works by donating energy stored within the molecule in processes catalyzed by enzymes. It is, therefore, a *coenzyme*.

The source of the energy stored in ATP is the breakdown of carbon-containing molecules from the food we eat (see *citric acid*). By a process called oxidative phosphorylation (see *cytochrome*), the energy of breakdown is utilized to link phosphate molecules to the adenine and sugar; that is, to the adenosine nucleoside. The removal of one phosphate from ATP in water under physiological conditions to form adenosine diphosphate (ADP) releases 7.3 kCal per mole (see Appendix 2). The removal of two phosphates to form adenosine monophosphate (AMP) releases a total of 7.7 kCal per mole.

ATP is neither the only method of storing energy for physiological purposes nor does it store as much energy as some other molecules. It is, however, the most common energy storage molecule in most living matter. Its structural formula is:

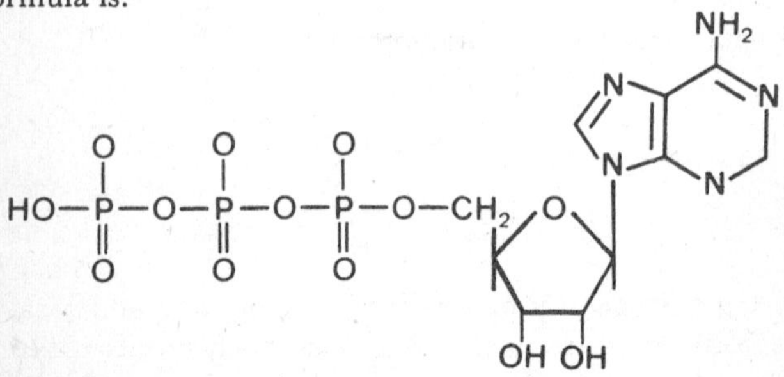

Adenyl cyclase

An *enzyme* catalyzing the breakdown of *adenosine triphosphate* into *cyclic adenosine monophosphate* to supply energy in muscles, liver and many other tissues. The enzyme is interesting because in muscles it is activated by the *hormone*, *adrenaline*, thus providing a molecular link between the hormone and the changes in cells which it brings about.

The enzyme molecule is probably bound to cellular membranes and does not occur free in the cell cytoplasm. It does not appear to function outside of cells.

Adrenaline (US: Epinephrine)

A *hormone* synthesized by the medulla, that is, the core, of the adrenal glands on top of the kidneys. Adrenaline is the principal component of a general behavioural response called the 'fight or flight' reaction. If an animal is endangered or surprised, the adrenal medullae secrete the hormone into the blood. Medullary cells respond to signals from the brain which arrive via the sympathetic nervous system (see *transmitter*). Thus, the hormone intensifies and sustains alertness that originates with sensations.

Adrenaline was isolated and identified in 1900. In a dog an injection of an extract of adrenal glands leads to an immediate, large but transient rise in blood pressure. This experiment constituted the first observation of a hormone in action.

The effects of adrenaline are rapid and widespread. *Glycogen* in liver and muscles is broken down to *glucose*, a major source of energy. Fat stores are also converted to energy. Peripheral blood vessels are constricted, but blood vessels in the heart, lungs and muscles dilate, leading to a rise in blood pressure, an increase in both breathing rate and amplitude and improved blood supply to muscles. Adrenaline also has a direct effect on heart muscle, causing it to contract and thus contributing to increased blood flow.

The molecular mechanism by which the hormone causes the breakdown of glycogen to glucose is well understood. Adrenaline activates the *enzyme*, *adenyl cyclase*, to convert *adenosine triphosphate* to *cyclic adenosine monophosphate*(cAMP). The cAMP in turn reacts with another enzyme, phosphorylase, which catalyzes the breaking of the bonds holding glucose molecules together to form glycogen. Thus, when the energy is needed, the hormone contributes to formation of cAMP. The cyclic adenosine monophosphate is called a 'second messenger', adrenaline being the first. It is probable that cAMP plays an analogous role with many other hormones.

The mechanisms underlying other functions of adrenaline are less clear. Its contradictory effects on blood vessels have been ascribed to the presence of *receptors* with opposing functions in the muscle cells regulating the sizes of peripheral vessels on the one hand and those in the heart and lungs on the other. These receptors have been labelled alpha and beta. In general alpha receptors are excitatory, causing muscles to contract, thus narrowing the blood vessels. (If the muscle is normally contracted as in a sphincter, excitatory receptors would cause it to relax.) Beta receptors may either excite or inhibit with the opposite effect. In particular, beta receptors in the heart are excitatory. See also *noradrenaline, transmitter*.

On the other hand, beta receptors in the lungs act according to the usual rules; that is, they inhibit muscle contraction. Thus in the lungs, adrenaline as a drug relaxes the bronchial air passages, and it can be used in nasal sprays to control asthmatic attacks. Because it is also a heart stimulant, however, adrenaline can cause dangerous side effects in asthmatics who also have heart disease. Drugs that act more selectively on *adrenergic* receptors in the bronchi are now more commonly used.

As a drug, adrenaline may also be used to control bleeding during superficial operations. Its excitatory effect causes constriction of peripheral blood vessels with a reduction in bleeding. The hormone cannot be used to control severe haemorrhage because of its contradictory action on the heart.

Adrenaline is synthesized in the adrenal medullae from *noradrenaline* , a transmitter of nerve signals in parts of the nervous system. Both adrenaline and noradrenaline and their precursors in the biosynthetic process, *dopa* and *dopamine*, are called *catecholamines*. The structural formula for adrenaline is:

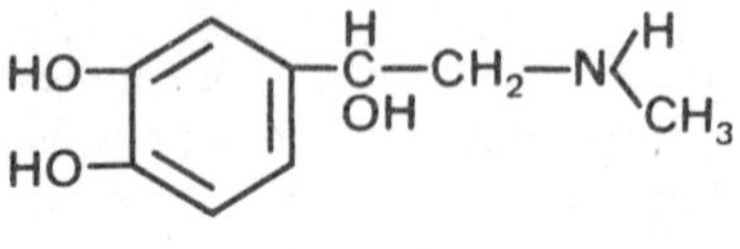

Adrenergic

Energized by *noradrenaline*. The word originated because it was believed that certain nerve cells or neurons release *adrenaline*. It is now recognized that nerve cells, in the sympathetic branch of the autonomic nervous system (see *transmitter*) and in parts of the brain, release noradrenaline rather than adrenaline. Noradrenaline is, therefore, a transmitter of signals from one nerve cell to the next and between some nerve cells and the muscles and glands those cells innervate. In other words, noradrenaline activates a nerve, muscle or glandular cell. Therefore, an adrenergic neuron is either one which releases noradrenaline when it signals or one which is energized by noradrenaline.

Adrenocorticotropic hormone (ACTH)

One of the *hormones* secreted by the pituitary gland encased in the bony roof of the mouth. ACTH circulates in the *blood* to reach its target organ, the cortex of the adrenal glands which are located one on top of each kidney. There, ACTH stimulates the synthesis and secretion of corticosteroid hormones, especially *hydrocortisone* and several closely related *steroids* including cortisone. The corticosteroids bolster the body's adjustment to stress, providing a more long-term action than, for example, *adrenaline*.

ACTH is secreted in response either to a negative feedback when the blood level of corticosteroids falls or to a direct command issued by the hypothalamus, a part of the mid-brain to which the pituitary is connected. The command takes the form of a *releasing factor*, a chemical secreted by nerve cells in the hypothalamus which reaches the pituitary via a local blood supply. The hypothalamus in turn responds to stress from either inside the body (e.g., a sudden fall in blood sugar) or outside it (for example, cold, burns or profound emotional disturbance).

ACTH is secreted by cells of the forward segment of the pituitary, the anterior pituitary or adenohypophysis. It is a polypeptide; that is, it consists of 39 *amino acids*. Amongst different animal species there are differences in the amino acids numbered 25 to 39, but the first 24 amino acids are the same in all species and produce all the known effects of the complete ACTH molecule. A synthetic drug consisting only of the first 33 amino acids may be used to overcome some pituitary deficiencies caused by diseases such as a pituitary tumour. ACTH may also be used as a drug to diagnose adrenal cortical deficiencies. In normal people, a dose of ACTH causes an immediate rise in blood levels of hydrocortisone which does not occur in patients whose adrenal cortex is malfunctioning.

The hormone works by stimulating *adenyl cyclase* to break down *adenosine triphosphate* to form *cyclic adenosine monophosphate*. This process both releases energy and activates an *enzyme*, phosphorylase, which catalyzes the breakdown of *glycogen* to *glucose*, a further source of energy. ACTH also stimulates the movement of glucose into adrenocortical cells from the blood and activates the breakdown of *cholesterol* in the adrenal glands from which other adrenocortical hormones can be synthesized. Thus, ACTH causes adrenocortical cells not merely to secrete their hormones but also to produce more of them.

Albumin (see *Blood*)

Alcohol dehydrogenase

An *enzyme* found in most organisms. Its roles differ greatly from organism to organism. For example, in yeast alcohol dehydrogenase converts acetaldehyde (*see ketone*) to ethyl alcohol, ethanol, at the end of the fermentation process. In human and other mammalian liver, a slightly different form of the same enzyme converts ethanol to acetaldehyde. Because the enzyme is a catalyst, it could be expected to assist a chemical reaction to move in either direction, and its role depends on the relative availability of substrate; i.e., ethanol or acetaldehyde. In theory, liver cells could produce alcohol, but only in a serious disease such as diabetes mellitus is the increase in the amount of available acetaldehyde likely to approach the necessary level, a condition which would be fatal.

In mammals the enzyme regulates the speed at which alcohol is removed from the *blood*. Clearance in humans is normally about 7 grams/per hour. Heavy drinkers may clear alcohol more rapidly because of an adaptive increase in the amount of alcohol dehydrogenase in their liver cells. That is, the presence of large amounts of ethanol causes liver cells to synthesize more of the enzyme. This remarkable phenomenon is seen in the synthesis of some other enzymes and is thought to be related to the functioning of the genes (see *deoxyribonucleic acid*), but the precise mechanism is not understood.

Acetaldehyde may be further broken down to acetic acid so that it becomes a source of energy. Thus alcohol produces about 7 kCal per gram, but it contains none of the essential nutrients such as vitamins. Acetaldehyde may also be converted in the liver to *fat*.

Aldosterone

A *hormone* secreted by the cortex of the adrenal glands on top of the kidneys. Aldosterone helps to regulate the *sodium* and *potassium* content of *body fluids*. It acts on kidney cells where it causes retention of sodium and an increased excretion of potassium.

Although aldosterone is synthesized by cells in the adrenal cortex, secretion is not regulated by the pituitary output of *adrenocorticotropic hormone*. A decrease in body fluid, or a decline in sodium or an increase in potassium content causes kidney cells to secrete an *enzyme, renin*, which catalyzes the splitting of a blood-plasma *protein*, angiotensinogen, producing another hormone, *angiotensin*. Angiotensin in turn stimulates the production of aldosterone! Thus, the feedback control over aldosterone biosynthesis involves its target organ, the kidney, but not a 'third party' – the brain, or the hypothalamus and pituitary.

Aldosterone is a *steroid* like *cholesterol* from which it is synthesized. It is designated a mineralocorticoid; that is, an adrenal cortical steroid which regulates minerals. It is distinguished from the glucocorticoids which regulate the use of *carbohydrates* including *glucose*, and of proteins. See *Hydrocortisone* for details of glucocorticoid activity.

Amino acid

A small, nitrogen-containing, acidic (see *acid*) molecule which is the constituent of *proteins*, many *hormones*, *transmitters* and other organic chemicals, all of which may be grouped together as polypeptides (see *peptide*). Nerve cells or neurons in particular must somehow determine whether certain amino acids are to be used as constituents of protein or converted into transmitters of nerve signals between neurons. The mechanism of this choice is not understood.

Amino acids are obtained from the breakdown of proteins in food during the digestive processes. Human cells can interconvert most amino acids, but eight are essential; that is, they cannot be synthesized by human cells in amounts that are adequate for the body's needs. Like *vitamins*, they must be obtained directly from the diet. The essential amino acids for humans are:

Methionine	Isoleucine
Tryptophan	Leucine
Threonine	Phenylalanine
Valine	Lysine

Note that the ending, —ine, denotes an amino acid or a chemical which contains an amide group (NH_2) such as *thyroxine*, but not all amino acids have this ending; for example, tryptophan.

Animal proteins such as meat, fish and eggs contain all the essential amino acids, but many vegetable proteins do not. For example, polished rice has almost no lysine. Potato and whole wheat lack methionine and lysine. Diets consisting exclusively of such foods can lead to severe protein-deficiency diseases such as kwashiorkor, especially in children who need protein for growth as well as body maintenance. Lack of tryptophan may be a contributing factor in the *niacin*-deficiency disease, pellagra.

Phenylketonuria is a serious disease of infants caused by the inherited inability to break down the essential amino acid, phenylalanine. The *enzyme* required to break down phenylalanine is missing in these people. Children at risk can be identified by a simple biochemical test, however, and the disease can be controlled during the crucial early period of development by a diet that is low in phenylalanine-containing proteins. (See also *gamma-amino butyric acid, glutamic acid, glycine*.)

Amylase

An *enzyme* which exists in more than one form in the digestive tract. As alpha-amylase, it is important for the digestion of starch.

Alpha-amylase is a constituent of *saliva* where it is known by its former name, ptyalin. It is also secreted into the intestine by the pancreas.

Under physiological conditions of temperature and acid-base balance, amylase catalyzes the splitting of the starch molecule into digestible *sugars*. Starch is the plant storage form of *carbohydrate* analogous to *glycogen* in animals.

Androgen

A male sex *hormone*. In addition to *testosterone*, natural androgens include androsterone and dehydro-epiandrosterone.

Both the natural androgens and synthetic analogues may be used to maintain male secondary characteristics such as body-hair distribution and muscle development even after malfunction or loss of the testes. Synthetic androgens are used to treat osteoporosis, an abnormal loss of *calcium* from *bone*, and they have also been effective in the treatment, though unfortunately not the cure, of breast cancer. The anabolic *steroids* used by athletes to increase musculature, often illegally and with a risk of temporary sterility, are androgens.

All of the natural androgens are *steroids*. They are synthesized by cells in the adrenal cortex of women as well as men, and of course by the testes.

Angiotensin

Two *hormones*: angiotensin I and angiotensin II. The latter has the most important physiological effects. It causes the cortex of the adrenal glands on top of the kidneys to secrete *aldosterone*. Aldosterone in turn affects the regulation of *electrolyte* balance in *body fluids* by the kidneys. Angiotensin probably also helps to regulate blood pressure.

Angiotensin I is formed from a *protein*, angiotensinogen, found normally in the *blood*, by means of catalytic action of an *enzyme, renin*. Angiotensin II is formed when another enzyme, converting enzyme, removes two *amino acids* from angiotensin I. The action of renin is dependent on loss of *sodium ions* from the blood, or it may be promoted by haemorrhage and a fall in blood pressure. Angiotensin II acts both indirectly through aldosterone and probably directly by constricting blood vessels to increase blood pressure, blood volume and sodium retention. It is scarcely surprising that a chemical with such diverse actions should be the product of a complex biosynthetic pathway. This cascade technique of self-protection against accidental synthesis of a powerful chemical is probably common in the body; see for example, *blood factor*.

The molecular mechanism by means of which angiotensin alters the behaviour of cells in the adrenal cortex and blood vessels is not understood. As a drug, the hormone is the most powerful constrictor of blood vessels available. It may be used to raise blood pressure, but side effects arising out of the complex cardiovascular control system limit its value. More selective synthetic drugs are usually preferred.

Antibody

A *protein* molecule, one of a class of immunoglobulins synthesized by cells of the immune defence system including lymphocytes and plasma cells in the *lymph* nodes and the pancreas. The remarkable feature of an antibody is that its synthesis is stimulated by the presence of a foreign substance, an *antigen*, which the antibody is specifically designed to attack and immobilize. Each antibody attacks only one or at most a very small number of structurally similar antigens.

When the antigen first appears, plasma cells need about a week to produce the appropriate antibody, but once a group of plasma cells have learned how to synthesize an antibody, the cells multiply. The resultant clone of cells able to synthesize that one antibody is then available immediately if the triggering antigen reappears. That is why people get measles only once, for example. During the illness, plasma cells are acquiring the capacity to synthesize the correct antibody. The next time the measles antigen appears, these 'educated' plasma cells are ready and waiting.

Why then can we catch several colds in one winter? The short answer is: we do not know. But there is some relevant data. There are many different viruses which produce the common cold. At any one time, 15 such viruses can be found in the London air. Each one contains different antigens. In addition some antigens seem to be 'stronger' than others. They guarantee a permanent population of plasma cells able to synthesize antibodies against them. Other antigens are weaker.

On the face of it, antibody response to serious diseases might be expected to be more certain than the response to less serious conditions like a cold. Unfortunately, this is not true. For example, there is evidence that cancer cells contain antigens which are actually foreign to the patient's body. Yet it has not been possible to demonstrate a consistent antibody response against cancer antigens.

The antibody–antigen relationship also underlies the condition known as allergy. Allergy antigens are foreign substances like pollen, house dust or even penicillin. They cause plasma cells to synthesize antibodies in the same way as the antigen in a disease-causing substance. All antibodies may indirectly evoke inflammatory responses like fever and a runny nose (see *histamine, leukotriene, prostaglandin*). They are means of ridding the body of an invasive substance and are therefore useful if the antigen is dangerous, but inflammatory responses are a nuisance if the cause is innocuous. Indeed, if the inflammatory response is very strong as in asthma, for example, the antibodies themselves are dangerous.

Antibodies also raise a serious theoretical question about the nature of protein synthesis. In theory, each protein synthesized in the body is formed on a template which is in turn the chemical copy of a gene (see *deoxyribonucleic acid*

(DNA), *ribonucleic acid*). Does this mean that each of us contains within our chromosomes a gene for every possible antibody? It seems unlikely because like the number of antigens, the variety of antibodies is vast if not infinite. Various mechanisms have been suggested to solve the problem: first, mutations – called point mutations – take place in the genes carried by antibody-synthesizing cells in the course of the generation of new cells during the life of the individual. Point mutations occur when there is a change in only one DNA *base*. But this mutation mechanism obviously implies a large element of chance. Second, somatic selection, the process of evolution hypothesized by Darwin, may also apply at the cellular level. Plasma cells synthesize antibodies in the presence of antigen. Those capable of producing the necessary antibody generate new cells whereas others are disabled or destroyed by the antigen. Such a process would be enormously wasteful, though that is by no means proof against it. Third, mutations may involve larger pieces of the gene. Indeed, there is evidence that DNA or the proteins associated with it contain control mechanisms that could regulate this form of mutation in terms of environmental circumstances such as the presence of an antigen, but the evidence is highly controversial. In any case, the variability of antibodies is one of the important unsolved problems of biochemistry.

Each antibody has a well-defined general structure:

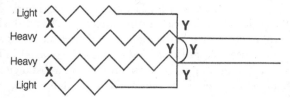

The zigzag wavy lines represent segments of the molecule that vary from antibody to antibody, giving the necessary specificity against one or a very few antigens. The straight lines represent the same sequences of *amino acids* repeated in all antibodies formed by plasma cells in one person. Many of these sequences are identical within a species, and some are repeated in related species. The two outer chains of amino acids, marked 'light', are smaller and lighter in weight than the much longer chains marked 'heavy'. The lines labelled Y are di-sulphide bridges consisting of two atoms of *sulphur*. Each bridge holds two chains together. The spaces labelled X are the binding sites where the antibody combines with the antigen to immobilize it. In human antibodies, there are two kinds of light chain distinguished by their invariant sequences and three different kinds of heavy chains. The latter three determine the class of immunoglobulin into which the antibody falls. There are at least 40 different species of light chain within the basic two, moreover, so that variability in the constant structure also occurs. Such variables are themselves antigenic in other bodies, and like *blood groups*, they are part of the system of tissue types which must be matched if transplant surgery is to succeed.

Antidiuretic hormone (ADH) (see *Vasopressin*)

Antigen

Any substance foreign to an organism which causes the organism to produce *antibodies* against it. Under certain conditions, however, an antigen may cause an organism to develop immunological tolerance towards it. Immunological tolerance is a condition in which the organism does not develop an antibody against the antigen. Either one of two conditions may explain tolerance:

(1) In the foetus or in early infancy the individual is exposed to the antigen. At this time its immune defence system is still developing so that the foreign substance becomes identified by antibody-forming plasma cells in the *lymph* nodes and pancreas and in the thymus gland (see *hormone*) as a self-like substance, as though it had been a part of the body.

(2) In an adult either a very low dose or a very high dose of an antigen – but not a 'moderate' dose – can produce tolerance, but it lasts only as long as the antigen remains in

the body. The mechanism of this form of tolerance is not clear.

In some people, early foetal and post-natal identification of self-antigens is incomplete, or the identification may fail with respect to one self-antigen later in life. Such a later failure could be the result of an infection in which a bacterial toxin, for example, damages the self-antigenic molecule so that it can no longer be 'recognized' by plasma cells. Some such process is thought to occur during scarlet fever in some patients. The disease itself can be cured with antibiotic drugs, but a few people later develop a heart disease, rheumatic fever, which seems to have been caused by antibodies which attack self-antigens in the patient's heart muscle. Rheumatic fever is called an autoimmune disease. Some forms of cancer and both early- and late-onset diabetes (see *insulin*) may be autoimmune diseases.

Most antigens are *proteins*, but complex *sugars*, polysaccharides, may also be antigenic. Some small molecules called haptens are capable of initiating an immune response if they have first combined with a larger molecule, called a carrier, which may not itself be antigenic. Some bacterial antigens are actually haptenic; that is, a molecule in the wall surrounding a bacterium becomes an antigen only after it has combined with a carrier in the patient's *blood*. Note that the carrier is modified by the hapten in a manner which causes an autoimmune reaction. Many allergies are thought to be the result of such reactions.

Apatite (see *Bone, Calcium, Phosphorus*)

Aqueous humour (see *Vitreous humour*)

Ascorbic acid

Vitamin C, the antiscorbutic vitamin; that is, it prevents scurvy. Ascorbic acid plays an important but poorly understood role in cellular energy storage. It also functions as a cofactor (see *coenzyme*) in *iron* absorption, *noradrenaline* synthesis and *steroid* production, and it contributes to the immune defences of the body.

Scurvy is chiefly a reflection of malformed connective tissue and *bone* caused by the defective synthesis of *collagen*, an important structural *protein*. Ascorbic acid plays an essential role in collagen synthesis. It is required in the biological transformation of one *amino acid*, tyrosine, to one of the essential amino acids, tryptophan, and it plays a role in the biosynthesis of sugar-amines; that is, molecules consisting of a *sugar* and an amino acid. In the absence of ascorbic acid, wounds heal slowly and incompletely. Bones are thinner and more brittle. Bleeding may reflect a weakening of blood vessels because of defective collagen synthesis, but it may also be caused by the failure of cells to convert the B vitamin, *folic acid*, to an active form. Ascorbic acid is required in this process, too. If ascorbic acid deprivation continues, scurvy can be fatal, usually because of haemorrhage.

Excepting the bone malformation, symptoms of scurvy rapidly respond to doses of vitamin C. It is obtained from fresh fruits and vegetables. Black currants and strawberries actually contain more than citrus fruits, but oranges, lemons, grapefruit and even tangerines are more consistently available. Cooking and storage disperse or destroy ascorbic acid, and packaged fruit juices contain variable amounts of the vitamin.

Although a reasonably balanced and properly cooked diet supplies average needs, supplements may be required if wounds are healing, for example. Some highly reputable scientists have believed that large doses of ascorbic acid can prevent or reduce the symptoms of colds, but there is little evidence supporting them. It has also been suggested that vitamin C may control symptoms of schizophrenia and even of cancer, but again, the evidence has not yet justified the hope.

Like most other organic molecules, ascorbic acid comes in two forms: L from laevo or left and D from dextro or right. Crystals of the respective molecules cause polarized light to be bent either to the left or to the right. Only

L-ascorbic acid is biologically active. Most higher plants and animals can synthesize their own vitamin C from glucose. Guinea pigs and the primates, including man, lack the *enzyme* which catalyzes the final step in the synthetic process. The structural formula of L-ascorbic acid is:

$$
\begin{array}{l}
O\!=\!C \!-\!\rule[0.5ex]{0pt}{0pt} \\
HO\!-\!C \!-\!\rule[0.5ex]{0pt}{0pt} \\
\qquad \| \quad O \\
HO\!-\!C \!-\!\rule[0.5ex]{0pt}{0pt} \\
H\!-\!C \!-\! \\
HO\!-\!C\!-\!H \\
\quad CH_2OH
\end{array}
$$

Base

(1) A substance which combines with an *acid* to produce a *salt* and water.

(2) A substance which accepts protons or one which gives up hydroxyl (OH) *ions* in water. In this sense, a base is 'basic' and tends to elevate pH (see Appendix 2) above 7. It may also be looked upon as the opposite of an acid in that a base forms a compound with an acid donating electrons whereas an acid forms a compound with a base by accepting electrons from the base.

(3) A molecule or an ion which possesses the property of combining loosely with a proton, usually a *hydrogen* ion, to form a hydrogen bond (see Appendix 3). Thus *adenine*, *cytosine*, *guanine* and *thymine* are bases in *deoxyribonucleic acid* and *uracil* replaces thymine in *ribonucleic acid*. Adenine is also a base in *adenosine triphosphate* and *cyclic adenosine monophosphate* and the other nucleic acid bases similarly enter into *nucleotides*. All of these bases owe their properties to *oxygen* atoms, but a *nitrogen* atom may serve the same purpose in other bases.

Bicarbonate (see *Carbonic acid*)

Bile

The secretion of the liver which functions in digestion and excretion. Bile is normally brown to yellow, but it may become greenish. It is an oily, viscous, alkaline fluid with a bitter taste.

Liver cells secrete about a litre of bile per day. It is stored in the gall bladder where much of the water is removed so that it becomes concentrated. *Fat* in the duodenum, the upper part of the small intestine nearest to the stomach, stimulates synthesis of a *hormone*, cholecystokinin, by the small intestine. Cholecystokinin causes the gall bladder to contract, discharging bile into the duodenum. Although its alkalinity tends to counteract stomach acids (see *hydrochloric acid*) and probably assists food absorption generally, the principal role of bile is in fat absorption.

Fats are insoluble in water and are, therefore, not easily absorbed into cells. Bile assists absorption. From the standpoint of digestion, the active ingredients of bile are the bile salts, glycocholate and taurocholate, both *steroids* with amphipathic characteristics; that is, each molecule contains arrangements of atoms such that one side of the molecule rejects water and the other side tends to dissolve in it (see *lipid*). In a watery environment such as the interior of the small intestine, bile salts form micelles, globular capsules one molecule thick the outsides of which are hydrophilic. The micelle wall may also contain other fatty molecules with similar properties. Micelles contribute to the emulsification of fats because the hydrophobic interiors of the micelles are a suitable environment for the tiny particles of fat broken down from food in the stomach. The micelles can be reabsorbed through the intestinal walls where they mix with the watery *lymph* and are distributed throughout the body. Each micelle may contain as little as a single molecule, for example, of *cholesterol* or of the fat-soluble *vitamins*, A, D or K. In the absence of bile salts, neither these vitamins nor any fats are adequately absorbed.

The bile salts are formed in the liver from cholesterol, first as bile acids, especially cholic acid, deoxycholic acid and chenocholic acid. They do not persist in bile, though

cholesterol itself may be mixed with the bile salts. Bile acids
are converted to the salts by combination with the amino
acids, glycine or taurine.

Bile also contains pigments, especially bilirubin. The
liver is one of the principal loci for the breakdown of
haemoglobin, the ultimate breakdown products of which
include the pigments. The reddish brown of bilirubin (L.:
ruber = red) gives its normal colour to faeces. The smell is
due both to the bile pigments and to the bacteria which
normally inhabit the intestines, often contributing to the
digestive process. In the faeces, bile also carries out of the
body some fats and bile salts as well as many drugs which
have been broken down in the liver.

If the excretion of bile pigments into the intestines should
be impeded, they may build up in the blood causing the
yellow discoloration of skin and *mucous* membranes recognized as jaundice. The yellowing can also reflect excessive
bile pigment formation as may happen in certain forms of
anaemia arising from abnormal breakdown of red blood
cells. Jaundice usually reflects either a liver disorder caused
by an infection or by obstructions in the liver or in the ducts
leading to the gall bladder or the intestines. Any of these
conditions may be serious, and jaundice is always a sign
that medical attention is essential.

Blood

A tissue, like skin and *bone*, consisting of formed elements in
an unorganized ground substance with the difference that
the ground substance of blood, plasma, is a liquid under
normal conditions. The function of blood is transportation
of *antibodies*, *hormones*, *oxygen* and substances obtained from
food throughout the body and the removal of *carbon dioxide*
and waste materials to the excretory organs. An adult has
about five litres of blood.

The formed elements are the red blood cells also called
erythrocytes (Gr.: *erythros* = red + *kytos* = cell), white cells
or leukocytes (Gr.: *leukos* = white) and platelets. White cells

are actually translucent. Red blood cells represent about 45 per cent of the blood by volume, and of course they give blood its characteristic colour. Both the arterial red and the venous bluish-red derive from the *haemoglobin* molecule inside the cell which carries the gaseous oxygen. Red blood cell deficiencies, the anaemias, are described under *cyanocobalamin*, *haemoglobin* and *iron*. Erythrocytes are formed in the bone marrow by division from unspecialized stem cells. They have no nuclei and cannot reproduce themselves. On average, blood contains about five million red cells per litre. The actual number is regulated by a hormone, *erythropoietin*. In conditions of relative oxygen shortage such as occur in certain lung disorders or at high altitudes, more erythropoietin is secreted and the number of red blood cells increases. The average life of erythrocytes is normally 120 days. They are destroyed in the capillaries, heart, liver and especially, the spleen.

There are three varieties of white cells: granular (so-called because when they are stained, they contain many dark grains), lymphocytes and monocytes. All three are instrumental parts of the immune defence system, but not all of their functions are fully understood.

The granular cells are themselves divided into three subcategories on the basis of their reactions to the dyes used to make them visible under the microscope: neutrophil, the most common; eosinophil, so named because they are stained red by eosin; and basophil which are stained by methylene blue and are the rarest white cells. Granular cells are also called collectively polymorphonuclear leucocytes because their cell nuclei contain many lobes. They are formed in bone marrow from the same stem cells as erythrocytes. Their life span is measured in hours rather than days. The factors determining whether stem cells become erythrocytes or some other kind of blood cell are not understood.

Neutrophils ingest and destroy bacteria. With eosinophils which are involved in allergic reactions and the destruction of certain parasites, the neutrophils are also called phagocytes (Gr.: *phage* = to eat). Basophils may also be called mast cells and contain *heparin, histamine* and *serotonin*. The presence of histamine implies that basophils take part in inflammatory reactions (see *antibody, hyaluronic acid, leukotriene, prostaglandin*).

Lymphocytes are formed principally in the thymus gland below the thyroid in the upper chest, in the spleen and the *lymph* nodes, although some may also be produced in bone marrow. With the plasma cells, they recognize *antigens*, synthesize antibodies against them, and they may also act as phagocytes. Whereas granular cells assemble rapidly at points of damage or injury as a first line of defence, lymphocytes act more slowly. From the standpoint of their life span, there are two varieties of lymphocytes: short (two or three days) and long (up to 200 days). Other classificatory criteria are described under *lymph*.

Monocytes are also formed in bone marrow and in the spleen. They are phagocytic, but their function is otherwise unclear. The white cells are larger than red blood cells, and monocytes are the largest.

Leukemia is a general term for uncontrolled proliferation of leukocytes, the granular white cells. It is a kind of cancer. Uncontrolled proliferation of lymphocytes occurs in Hodgkin's disease. Leukopenia is a shortage of white cells, and the complete absence of granular cells, a rare condition, is called agranulocytosis. Though they are all seriously disabling diseases which may be fatal, their causes are not understood.

The third formed element in the blood, the platelets or thrombocytes (Gr.: *thrombo* = lump, clot), are essential for the formation of a blood clot. They are pieces of the large stem cells in bone marrow and may also be formed in the lungs. They are the smallest of the formed elements, and like erythrocytes, they have no nuclei. When a blood vessel is damaged, platelets aggregate at the site. The physical causes of this reaction, the first stage in blood coagulation, are not clear, but it may be associated with a prostaglandin-like substance, thromboxane A_2. Platelets contain at least four of the *blood factors* and *adrenaline, noradrenaline* and *serotonin*. Platelets are also aggregated by *collagen* and are believed to be instrumental in the roughening of artery walls leading to hardening of the arteries (arteriosclerosis) and high blood pressure.

Blood plasma is a sticky, yellowish liquid with a characteristically sweet smell. Its principal constituents are water in which *proteins* are dissolved along with *salt*, *glucose* and substances being transported from one part of the body to another such as hormones. The plasma proteins play several roles and are of three main types: albumin, *globulin* and fibrinogen (see *blood factor*). All are large molecules and unlike other plasma constituents, they cannot pass through capillary walls under normal conditions. Indeed, even white cells can escape through vessel walls though they are larger than proteins, but the latter are retained in part because of their electrical properties (see *electrolyte*). The effect of the proteins and other non-aqueous molecules in plasma is to maintain an osmotic pressure from the tissues to the blood which counteracts the movement of plasma fluid into the tissues under the pressure of the heart beats. The osmotic pressure of the plasma helps to maintain blood volume. If it is reversed because of disease, or if blood pressure falls abnormally, fluid builds up in the tissues, a condition known as oedema.

The albumins are the most abundant of the plasma proteins. They act as carriers for many other body chemicals such as hormones and *lipids*, for many drugs and for the foreign haptens which may then become antigenic. Albumins are formed in the liver.

There are four major groups of globulins: alpha 1, alpha 2, beta and gamma. Gamma globulins are also called immunoglobulins. The first three are formed in the liver, and the immunoglobulins are formed by lymphocytes and plasma cells and include all known antibodies. For more detailed descriptions, see *globulins*.

Fibrinogen, the third plasma protein, reacts with thrombin under the influence of chemicals from platelets to form fibrin, a long, stringy protein which ties the platelets together in a lattice. This is the actual blood clot.

See also *blood group*.

Blood factor

Also called coagulation factor. One of twelve or thirteen substances, probably all *proteins*, in the *blood*, or blood vessel walls which are necessary to form a blood clot.

The clotting process must somehow be kept under the most delicate control. In the event of injury to a blood vessel, a clot must form quickly to prevent haemorrhage, but under normal circumstances, the blood must flow freely. Untimely clots can block blood vessels with severe damage to the surrounding tissue because of the loss of *oxygen* and other nutrients and the build up of wastes which become toxic in large quantities. If the blockage occurs in the heart or brain, death can follow rapidly. The biological response to these potentially contradictory needs is a sequence of blood factors, each one formed from a preceding factor. The process is often called a cascade.

There are eight steps in the clotting cascade, not all of them yet fully understood:

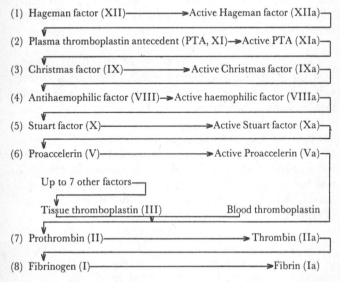

Factor IV is *calcium* which is required to obtain the chemical conversions in steps 3, 4, 5, 6 and 7. Christmas,

Hageman and Stuart are the names of patients who suffered from blood diseases which were traced to the absence of the respective factors. Haemophilia may be due to the absence of Christmas factor (IX), but the cause is more often the absence of Factor VIII. The absence of a blood factor probably reflects a genetic error (see *deoxyribonucleic acid*) which may be inherited.

In addition to the cascade shown above, a factor to stabilize the clot, fibrin stabilizing factor, has been numbered XIII. The clot may be liquefied again, moreover, by plasmin which dissolves fibrin. Plasmin is formed in its turn from plasminogen.

The most important question mark remaining in the study of blood clotting is how damage to a blood vessel initiates step 1 in the cascade. The other steps, including the poorly understood formation of thromboplastin in both the blood and other tissues, could be the result of a disturbance of preset balances: thus, an excess of IXa causes the breakdown of VIII, and so on.

Blood group

The *antigens* in the membrane surrounding red blood cells. There are at least 14 different blood group systems, or antigenic systems, to which each of us belongs. The most important are the ABO and the rhesus (Rh) systems.

The ABO system was described by Karl Landsteiner, a Viennese biologist, in 1900. Landsteiner actually first identified the *antibodies* in human *blood* serum (that is, plasma without fibrinogen; see *blood factor*) against the antigens rather than the antigens themselves.

Blood group	Antigen in red cells	Antibodies in blood serum
AB	A and B	Neither
A	A	Anti-B
B	B	Anti-A
O	Neither	Both anti-A and anti-B

A antigens are subdivided into four groups: A_1, A_2, A_3 and A_4. Together, they are the blood group of about 44 per cent of white people in the United Kingdom. About 9 per cent are B group and 47 per cent are O group. People in the O group have neither the A nor the B antigen in their red blood cell membranes, but they probably have another related antigen called H which may also occur in the membranes of red blood cells in the AB, A and B groups, though less frequently. All ABO groups, furthermore, will have antigens in their red blood cell membranes from other blood group systems.

In 1940 Landsteiner and Wiener identified the rhesus blood group system in the blood of rhesus monkeys, and subsequently in human blood. There are some six Rh antigens, but only one, D, is important. About 85 per cent of people in the United Kingdom carry the D antigen. They are rhesus positive (Rh+). The remaining 15 per cent are rhesus negative (Rh−).

The relevance of blood groups to medicine appears in three circumstances: (1) transfusion, (2) pregnancy, and (3) organ transplants. Blood transfusion was attempted for a generation before the identification of the ABO system, often with severe allergy-like reactions which could be fatal. If the wrong blood group is transfused, the new cells will be attacked by antibodies in the recipient's blood. They may be broken up, but usually they are simply removed to the spleen or the liver and degraded. The patient may suffer fever and the symptoms of anaemia. In transfusions, the Rh and other blood groups are less important.

In pregnancy, the Rh system becomes the most significant. ABO incompatibilities between mother and foetus are common, but blood cells are too large to cross the placenta, and usually the mother's antibodies are not brought into contact with foetal antigens.

The effect of an Rh incompatibility between mother and foetus is likely to be more distressing because the infant is born live at full term and only then are the effects of the discrepancy observed. If an Rh− woman marries an Rh+ man, for example, there is a high probability that the children will be Rh+. No difficulty arises during pregnancy because the foetal blood cells do not cross the placenta, and unless she has received a transfusion of Rh+ blood in the past, the mother's blood will not contain anti-Rh+ or anti-D antibodies. During birth, however, the baby often bleeds through the placenta, and the mother may receive some of the foetal blood cells into her blood. She will then develop antibodies against them. If a later child is Rh+, there is a risk that antibodies from the mother's blood will attack the foetus. The child may be born with heart failure brought on by anaemia and may die within days. Some develop jaundice because the broken blood cells allow the formation of excessive *bile* pigments. This jaundice may be controlled with drugs that can neutralize the pigments, but there is a danger that the bile pigments will have damaged the developing nervous system so that the infant's brain is permanently damaged.

There are two kinds of therapy. Until recently, the most common was exchange transfusion. Immediately after birth, the Rh+ infant blood is drawn off and simultaneously replaced by Rh− blood. This serves to remove the excess bile pigments and enough of the Rh+ red cells to reduce the damage to acceptable levels.

It is also possible to inoculate an Rh− mother with anti-D antibodies which gives her an immunity against Rh+ blood so that she does not develop antibodies of her own against an Rh+ child. The inoculation is carried out immediately after the birth of the first Rh+ child and neutralizes any Rh+ cells from the infant that have got into the mother's blood. Inoculation is the most common procedure today, but because the foreign antibodies do not stay in the mother's blood, she is not permanently immune to Rh+ blood. Inoculation probably should be repeated after each birth.

In organ transplantation, compatibility of blood groups is one of the prerequisites for a satisfactory outcome. After all, blood transfusion is a kind of transplantation, but the transplanted tissue is also the one containing the blood group antigens. When transplantation involves another tissue, for example, the kidneys, the antigenic characteristics of that tissue must also be matched as closely as possible.

With the possible exception of identical twins, however, no two individuals have the same antigenic profiles. The blood-group antigens are mucopolysaccharides, chemicals consisting of several *sugars* and a fatty, mucous-like molecule. It is probable that they are not directly shaped by the genes because only proteins are formed on the nucleic acid template which originates in *deoxyribonucleic acid*. That is why it is possible to match the blood groups with comparative ease despite the variations amongst them. Antigens in other cells are often proteins to which a *carbohydrate* may be added. They are more closely specified structurally by the individual's genes. Tissue-typing has become more subtle as more has been learned, but it is still a lengthy process which can never be quite complete in the present state of the art.

Body elements

The elements, basic building blocks of matter, found in the body. Though most of the body is water, the figure is closer to 80 per cent than the common estimate of 96 per cent. Water is, of course, *hydrogen* and *oxygen*, and these two elements are the most frequently found atoms in all living matter. *Carbon* combines with other elements to make more compounds than do all the elements taken together. Without *nitrogen*, moreover, *protein* could not exist. These are the big four, but there are some 20 elements in the body. The following table is arranged by percentage of wet weight:

Oxygen	65%	Phosphorus	1.0	Magnesium	.05	Zinc	Trace
Carbon	18	Potassium	.35	Iron	.004	Fluorine	Trace
Hydrogen	10	Sulphur	.25	Iodine	.00004	Molybdenum	Trace
Nitrogen	3	Sodium	.15	Copper	Trace	Cobalt	Trace
Calcium	1.5	Chlorine	.15	Manganese	Trace	Vanadium	Trace

The most common body elements occur early in the Periodic Table of the Elements (see Appendix 3) and are very light. Indeed, the heaviest is iodine (atomic number: 53). Heavy elements such as lead (atomic number: 82) are often poisons.

Body fluids

The water-based tissues and locally-secreted liquids of the body. *Blood, lymph, mucus* and *semen* are tissues because they normally contain cells which are essential to their functions. *Cerebrospinal fluid* (CSF), *saliva, sweat, synovial fluid* and *tears* are locally-secreted liquids. Urine is *also* a locally-secreted liquid (see *renin, urea, uric acid*).

About 67 per cent of all body liquid by weight is contained inside cells. Intracellular fluid is part of the solid tissue such as nerve, muscle and *bone*. Its content of *protein, carbohydrate, fat, minerals* and other *electrolytes* is in constant flux depending on the state of the cell.

The body fluids as defined above represent all other liquids, and they are usually described under two heads: blood, which contains about 6 per cent of the total, and interstitial fluid – that which is between the tissues – including the remaining 27 per cent. Cerebrospinal fluid and synovial fluid are contained within partitions which confine them to restricted areas.

The content of interstitial fluid is also variable depending on the state of the body. It carries nutrients and wastes and all of the substances required by but not necessarily synthesized in all cells. The movement of substances into and out of interstitial fluid, is by diffusion or osmosis from the blood on the one hand, and the cells of solid tissues on the other. Active movement of molecules is also possible; for example, when cell membrane constituents pump substances into or out of cells. Indeed, the amount of interstitial fluid and blood is variable depending on the relative osmotic pressure between them, though any significant change in quantity may be a sign of disease. Intracellular fluid content is relatively invariable.

See also *acid, base, ion* and Appendix 2.

Bone

The tissue which forms the skeleton. Bone is a form of connective tissue consisting of about 70 per cent *mineral* crystals and 30 per cent organic matter, principally the *protein, collagen.*

Bone is not normally a dead material. It is formed and dissolved or resorbed by cells on its surface, and it is vascular in different degrees depending on the kind of bone. Throughout life, the remodelling of bone continues. Bones change shape and size both because they grow, and because they may undergo unusual stresses. Brittleness characteristic of bone in old age is due to the loss of organic material. On the other hand, the suppleness of long bones in the infant reflects the absence of mineral crystals.

With two exceptions, the clavicle and the large bones of the skull, bones are modelled first in the foetus as cartilage. Cartilage too is a connective tissue consisting primarily of collagen, but it is not just young bone. Unlike bone, cartilage is non-vascular so that the few cells inside it must be fed by diffusion. As the skeleton grows, cartilage is replaced by bone which is made up of three kinds of cells, all of them descendants of bone stem cells. Throughout life, the outer membrane or periosteum and the internal surfaces of bone are lined by stem cells. They give rise to osteoclasts, cells that dissolve both the organic and inorganic bone substance, osteoblasts which make new bone, and osteocytes or mature bone cells. Osteocytes are probably just osteoblasts which have encased themselves in mineral crystals. What is more, osteoclasts and osteoblasts may be the same cells performing different roles in response to the *hormones* then present and the availability of the relevant minerals; that is, *calcium* and *phosphorus* in the form of phosphate.

Growth is regulated by *growth hormone* and the sex hormones (see *oestrogen, progesterone, testosterone*). Ossification begins in the foetus with formation of true bone in a cartilagenous region. The cartilage is slowly absorbed and replaced by bone. At the ends of long bones, in the arms and legs, for example, separate bone structures form called epiphyses. The epiphyses become the protrusions to which the muscle sheaths are attached by means of tendons. The epiphyses grow separately from the long bones proper. Long bones grow both at the ends and on their outer surfaces, enlarging in length and thickness. This growth ceases when the cartilage between the epiphyses and the long bones proper is replaced by bone. Growth cessation is also hastened by the sex hormones, their function thus being apparently contradictory.

In the adult skeleton, cartilage has shrunk to a thin layer, but it still plays an important role. Especially in the joints and between spinal vertebrae, cartilage gives a smooth, compressible surface. Joint cartilage is called hyaline whereas the intervertebral cartilage is fibrous, there being slight differences in their composition. A third kind of cartilage, elastic, forms the outer ear.

Bone formation is also regulated by *parathormone* and *vitamin* D. Both act indirectly by regulating *blood* levels of calcium and phosphate, the combination of which is called apatite in bone. Vitamin D affects calcium absorption from food, and it is probably a cofactor with parathormone in the resorption of minerals from bone. Calcitonin, a hormone produced by the thyroid gland, appears to have an opposite effect, causing calcium to be removed from the blood and returned to bone.

Thus, in addition to its skeletal function, bone acts as a reservoir for two minerals which influence the acid-base balance of the *body fluids*. The amount of calcium and phosphate in the blood and tissues affects nervous activity, blood clotting and energy formation and storage throughout the body.

Bone also has a third role: it houses the machinery that turns out blood cells. The interior of long bones is porous or cancellous and contains highly vascular marrow where the blood cells mature. One large hole through the compact bone of the surface admits nerves and blood vessels serving the cancellous interior. Though it is hard and relatively non-porous, the surface is also traversed by fine tubes called Haversian canals (Clopton Havers, English physician, 1650–1702).

There are five types of bones in the skeleton: long bones, short bones, flat bones, sesamoid and supernumerary. Short bones form the feet and the flat of the hand. The toes are classified as short bones, but the fingers, as long bones. The skull, sternum, scapulae and parts of the pelvis and ribs are flat bones. Sesamoid bones are the small bones inside tendons that take great friction. The most important is the patella at the front of the knee. Supernumerary bones are epiphyses which have not formed a firm junction with their proximal long bones and are in a sense abnormal.

Like cartilage, bone is subject to damage and disease. The most obvious kind of damage is fracture, but bone abscesses and tumours also occur. Any bone disorder is hard to reach except by surgery because the tissue is rigid, and the relatively poor blood supply limits the effectiveness of drugs. Nerve cells run into the periosteum and the interiors of long bones, but they are not found inside compact bone.

Bradykinin

(Gr.: *bradys* = slow + *kinein* = to move)

A *hormone* formed from a *protein* in the *blood* which lowers blood pressure by dilating blood vessels and slowing heart beat while maintaining its strength. The blood vessels affected are the smallest arteries. Bradykinin is one of the most powerful vasodilators known. Because it works on tissue immediately beside its site of formation, bradykinin is called a local hormone.

It is a nonapeptide; that is, it consists of nine *amino acids*. The *enzyme*, *trypsin*, splits kallidinogen, one of the large blood proteins, to form bradykinin. Kallidinogen may be the same as alpha$_2$-*globulin*. In fact, it is split into kallidin, a decapeptide (10 amino acids) which then loses one amino acid to become bradykinin.

The hormone is also present in *saliva*, *sweat* and pancreatic juice. It is one of the active ingredients in the toxin injected by a wasp's sting and of some snake venoms. In both cases, it probably serves to dilate the blood vessels of the victims, thus hastening the toxic effect. The mechanism of action of bradykinin in cells of the heart and blood vessels is not known.

Calcitonin (See *Calcium*, *Hormone*)

Calcium (Ca)

The fifth most important *body element*, a *mineral* with important functions in diverse processes including tooth and *bone*
formation, blood clotting (see *blood factor*), muscle contraction and nerve cell signalling.

The absorption of calcium from food requires *vitamin* D.
The best sources of the mineral are cheese, milk, fish –
especially whitebait, smelts and sprats – watercress and
parsley.

Bone contains the largest calcium reservoir. A small
quantity, about 10 grams, remains in the blood, nervous
and muscle tissue. Calcium in combination with phosphates (see *phosphorus*) is deposited as apatite to harden
bone. The process begins in the foetus, but bone reshaping
goes on throughout life. Both during growth and in later
years, reshaping requires resorption of calcium from bone
into the blood and its redistribution. These processes are
regulated by vitamin D and two *hormones*, calcitonin and
parathormone. Calcitonin is formed in the thyroid gland at the
base of the neck. Parathormone is secreted by the parathyroid gland just behind the thyroid.

In the absence of vitamin D, children may develop rickets
with the improper growth of long bones. In adults the
analogous disorder, osteomalacia, produces a thinning of
the bones. An excess of vitamin D, on the other hand, may
cause deposition of calcium in other tissues, for example in
the form of stones in kidneys or other hollow organs.

Although calcitonin certainly affects calcium deposition,
no disease state related either to excess secretion or to
deficiency has been clearly identified. For the calcium-
related disorders resulting from parathyroid malfunction,
see *parathormone*.

In the blood-clotting process, calcium is identified as
factor IV. It is required as a cofactor to obtain the chemical
conversions in steps 3, 4, 5, 6 and 7.

Muscle contraction is brought about by two *proteins*, actin and *myosin*, within muscle cells. Calcium *ion* is an essential cofactor in the relative movement of these substances. Without it, muscle contraction would be slowed if it did not stop entirely.

Like muscle cells, nerve cells or neurons are excitable. The change in state from quiescent to active – that is, to contraction and signalling, respectively – is a response to electro-chemical changes within the cell membrane. Calcium ions both inside and outside the cell help to maintain membrane threshold at the correct physiological level. Calcium deficiency in the blood which may be caused by a failure in parathormone secretion, contributes to tetany, a condition in which muscle contraction in response to nerve signalling increases. The muscles twitch and go into spasms. In the disease called tetanus, similar spasms are caused by a bacterial toxin.

Calcium is the twentieth element in the Periodic Table (see Appendix 3) with an atomic weight of 40.08. Under physiological conditions in water, it typically occurs as a positive ion: Ca^{2+}.

Calculus (see *Saliva*)

Carbohydrate

A compound consisting of *carbon*, *hydrogen* and *oxygen* in which the latter two elements are usually in the proportion found in water; that is, two atoms of hydrogen to one of oxygen. Carbohydrates are found in all living cells. In animal cells, including those of humans, they are usually *sugars*. In plant cells, they may be starches, cellulose or gums as well as sugars. All carbohydrates originate in the green plants where they are synthesized from *carbon dioxide* and water using energy supplied by sunlight, and with the release of free oxygen.

In animals, carbohydrates are themselves the principal source of energy (see *citric acid, glucose*). The synthetic process found in plants is effectively reversed with the breakdown of carbohydrates in the presence of oxygen to carbon dioxide and water. Some energy can be obtained from the anaerobic (oxygen-lacking) breakdown of carbohydrates but not enough to sustain cellular activity for more than a short time. The aerobic combustion of one gram of carbohydrate yields 4.1 Calories.

Carbohydrates are classified as mono-, di-, tri- and polysaccharides (see *sugar*). The most important cellular source of energy is glucose, a monosaccharide. The human diet contains relatively little pure glucose, but it is a part of the three most important dietary disaccharides: *maltose*, sucrose and *lactose*. Maltose consists of two linked molecules of glucose and is the unit out of which starch is built. Sucrose, ordinary table sugar, consists of glucose and *fructose* and is most often obtained from cane sugar. Lactose is milk sugar. It is made up of glucose and *galactose*.

Both starch and cellulose are polysaccharides. We cannot digest cellulose because humans lack enzymes capable of breaking down its glucose units, but it is useful in the diet as fibre. Starch is, therefore, the most important source of glucose for energy. As we all know, excess glucose may be stored as *fat* to which it is converted in the body, but the most important storage form of sugar is a polysaccharide, *glycogen*, sometimes called animal starch. The major glycogen stores are in the liver and muscles. As blood-borne glucose is used up by cells, glycogen stores are broken down by the actions of *enzymes*. If the glycogen store happens to have been depleted by exercise, disease or starvation, fat stores and even *protein* may be converted to carbohydrates.

Many carbohydrates combine with proteins to form important structural elements, especially in cell membranes. Most *antigens*, for example, are thought to be glycoproteins. All *lipids*, moreover, are built up from glycerol, a carbohydrate, and fatty acids. Most of the lipid molecule is used in the process of conversion to glucose, but proteins contain *nitrogen* which is excreted as urea and thus lost to the body. Malnutrition or starvation first sap the carbohydrates stores followed by the fats, and ultimately, structural proteins and the enzymes that make life possible are destroyed.

Since virtually all carbohydrate is utilized as glucose, the dietary origin should not matter. There are in fact important practical considerations. Bread, for example, supplies *vitamins* and protein as well as carbohydrate. Milk contains *minerals*, vitamins, fats and proteins as well as lactose. Potatoes provide at least vitamin C in addition to carbohydrate. On the other hand, refined sugars and starches such as those commonly used in pastries offer few nutrients other than carbohydrate. They can be eliminated from most diets without damaging the health. There is also evidence that refined sugars contribute directly to diseases of the arteries and thus indirectly, to heart disease. Other carbohydrates have not been implicated. The reason for this distinction is not clear.

Carbon (C)

(L.: *carbo* = coal, charcoal)

The second most common *body element* by weight, carbon is a constituent of all organic compounds. Pure carbon is found naturally as diamond; coal and charcoal are almost pure. Though pure carbon may be useful as a drug to combat flatulence and to neutralize some poisons, it cannot be used by cells unless it is combined with *hydrogen* and *oxygen* in *carbohydrate*, *fat* or (with *nitrogen* too) *protein*. Obtained in these forms from food, carbon is an essential source of energy, part of the cell structure and of the enzymes that catalyze most biochemical transformations.

Because carbon is so widespread, no standard nutritional need has been fixed. A diet with insufficient carbon is tantamount to starvation. There is no disorder attributable to the malabsorption of carbon, but obviously, there is an almost infinite number of disturbances involving carbon compounds. Because carbon is absorbed only in combination with other atoms, moreover, an excessive dose of the pure substance might cause stomach upset, but it is not poisonous.

Carbon is a non-metallic solid with atomic number 6 and atomic weight, 12.011. The atom lacks four electrons in its outer ring and binds covalently to more elements than all other elements taken together (see Appendix 3).

Carbon dioxide (CO_2)

A colourless gas normally composing about 0.03 per cent of atmospheric air. Carbon dioxide is the universal waste product of the breakdown of carbon compounds in food by body cells to obtain energy. In plants, it is the source of *carbon* atoms which are built up using the energy of sunlight into the compounds in food.

Carbon dioxide is carried in the *blood* from the tissues to the lungs where it is breathed out and exchanged for *oxygen*. Only about a quarter of the blood CO_2 is carried by red blood cells. The remainder is transported by the plasma, a large part of it in the form of bicarbonate (see *carbonic acid*). Some CO_2 is simply dissolved in both the red blood cells and the plasma, and small quantities may be combined with *proteins*, especially *haemoglobin* which has released its oxygen. Concentration in venous blood is of course higher than in arterial blood, and more of the gas will be dissolved in the red blood cells and plasma. In the lungs, CO_2 diffuses through the capillary walls into the alveoli and thence into the air within these tiny sacks.

It is the presence of carbon dioxide in blood as much as oxygen lack which stimulates breathing. As carbonic acid or bicarbonate, carbon dioxide changes the acid–base balance of the blood. Sensory nerves in the brain stem and probably in the lungs respond to the CO_2 content, and when it rises, stimulate breathing. At concentrations over about 6 per cent, carbon dioxide is a poison.

Carbonic acid (H_2CO_3)

A weak *acid* formed from the combination of *carbon dioxide* and water, and from the combination of *hydrogen ions* (that is, a hydrogen atom without its electron) and bicarbonate ($H CO_3^-$), thus:

$$CO_2 + H_2O \rightleftharpoons H_2CO_3 \rightleftharpoons H^+ + HCO_3^-$$

Because blood plasma is largely water, the CO_2 carried by the blood may be carried as carbonic acid. However, under normal conditions of acid–base balance, or in the presence of normal *electrolytes*, carbonic acid dissociates into its components at the right of the formula. As a weak acid, carbonic acid in blood acts as a buffer; that is, because it dissociates into hydrogen ions which may be excreted in urine and a basic carbonate, it becomes necessary to add more acid to blood to lower its pH (see Appendix 2) significantly than would otherwise be the case. The reverse is also true, however; in the presence of a weak acid such as carbonic acid or of hydrogen ions, more alkali is needed significantly to raise pH. The presence or absence of carbonic acid is, therefore, of the greatest importance in the regulation of the acid–base balance of body fluids.

Both the formation of carbonic acid and its dissociation are catalyzed by an *enzyme*, carbonic anhydrase. The enzyme is present in red blood cells and in the cells lining kidney tubules, the working parts of the kidneys where water and electrolytes already filtered out of the blood are reabsorbed in accordance with the body's need to retain a normal acid–base balance. Formation or breakdown of carbonic acid in kidney tubule cells helps to regulate the excretion or absorption of other electrolytes such as *sodium* and *potassium*. (See also *aldosterone, angiotensin, renin*.)

Carboxypeptidase

An *enzyme* required for the digestion of *protein*. It is secreted by the pancreas and acts in the intestine.

There are two forms of the enzyme, A and B. Carboxypeptidase A is formed from a larger molecule, procarboxypeptidase, by the action of another enzyme, *trypsin*. The origin of carboxypeptidase B is less clear. The functions of the two enzymes differ in that they remove different *amino acids* from proteins, but both work at the carboxyl (COOH) terminal of the protein molecule (see Appendix 1).

Cartilage (see *Bone*)

Catecholamine

A molecule containing *nitrogen* and a benzene ring (see Appendix 1) to which two hydroxyl (OH) groups are attached. See also *adrenaline, dopa, dopamine, noradrenaline,* all of which are catecholamines.

Cerebrospinal fluid (CSF)

A part of the *body fluid* contained within a closed system of membranes surrounding and invaginating the brain and spinal cord. CSF is formed from the *blood* in the choroid plexuses, networks of fine blood vessels within the membrane system of the brain but not the spinal cord. It is reabsorbed into venous blood leaving the brain.

CSF has two functions: (1) it acts as a shock absorber for the delicate tissue of the central nervous system; (2) it mediates between blood and the central nervous system, carrying nutrients, gases, *electrolytes* and wastes.

Blood vessels within the brain bring blood to brain cells as they do in all other tissues, but cerebrospinal fluid is differently constituted. Its content is similar to plasma excepting that CSF contains a much smaller amount of *protein*; thus there is almost no fibrinogen (see *blood factor*) very few *globulins* and no *haemoglobin*. Increase in CSF protein may be a sign of serious infection such as meningitis, polio or syphilis. Because CSF is normally clear, moreover, any colour indicates the presence of a disorder. For example, redness is evidence of haemorrhage somewhere in the central nervous system. Small changes in *sugar*, protein or cellular content or in pressure may also indicate disease.

The brain and spinal cord are enclosed by three membranes, also called meninges. The outermost is the dura mater. Fluid, though not cerebrospinal fluid, separates it from the arachnoid mater. The pia mater closely surrounds the brain and spinal cord and is connected to the arachnoid by strands of the latter. The space between them is filled by CSF, and connects with four compartments within the brain itself. These are the two lateral ventricles, behind them the third ventricle, and behind and below, the fourth ventricle. The fourth ventricle is connected by fine tubes or foramina to the subarachnoid space and the central canal of the spinal cord. The cells of the choroid plexus which form CSF from blood plasma line the lateral ventricles, the fourth ventricle and the subarachnoid space surrounding the brain.

Disease, inflammation or damage caused by a tumour or a blow to the head can cause blockages, especially in the thin foramina. In infants whose skulls are still plastic, such blockages can cause hydrocephalus, the swelling of the skull. In adults, the blocked CSF builds up pressure which can lead to loss of consciousness and death. It is imperative to relieve pressure quickly either by injecting drugs that will stop or reverse CSF formation or surgically.

Chlorine (Cl)

(GR.: *chloros* = green)

An element with importance as a negative *ion* in *body fluids*. Chloride (Cl$^-$) is the principal source of the negative charge inside nerve and muscle cells which underlie their function (see *sodium*).

Chlorine is also required by cells in the stomach lining which synthesize *hydrochloric acid* (HCl). The most common chlorine compound in the body is ordinary table salt, NaCl.

In its natural state chlorine is a yellow-green gas used in warfare as poison gas but otherwise for fumigation and bleaching. Its atomic number is 17 and its atomic weight, 35.453. Chlorine is a halogen, one of four gases which form sodium salts. The others are fluorine, bromine and *iodine*.

Cholecystokinin (see *Bile*)

Cholesterol

A fat-like substance required in the body as a precursor of

bile salts, steroid hormones, the *myelin* sheaths surrounding the long processes of many nerve cells, and for energy formation. Cholesterol is also the principal constituent of gall stones and of deposits in arterial linings called atheromas. Atheromas are commonly found in the arteries of patients with high blood pressure and those who suffer a sudden, very painful heart attack, angina pectoris, or patients who have had a stroke.

Most people have about 140 gm or 5 oz of cholesterol in their bodies of which only four to six grams are in the blood. It is widely available in food, the most common sources being eggs (the yolk), butter, liver and cheeses. Lean meats contain about the same quantity as fat meat and chicken. The daily cholesterol intake varies with the individual diet, but because the liver synthesizes cholesterol, none at all is required.

In older people, there is a tendency for blood cholesterol quantity to rise. Otherwise the blood level remains remarkably even. Either the liver reduces its output or another balance is activated. Although blood cholesterol can be reduced temporarily by not eating high-cholesterol foods, liver synthesis soon increases to maintain the blood level. Evidently, cholesterol is too important in the body's economy to leave the amount available to chance – or dietary fashion!

Despite years of research, there is still no proof that high cholesterol intake leads to heart or arterial disease. What evidence there is comes from controversial statistics which link the chemical to heart disease according to some authorities. Low-fat and vegetarian diets often associated with a statistical reduction in cardiovascular disorders, especially by some American doctors, may also be aspects of changes in life-style which reduce tension and improve general health. The British Medical Association has not yet formally accepted that there is a connection between cholesterol intake and cardiovascular disease. Nevertheless, many people feel that while there is a risk, it is wise to exercise caution and to eat accordingly. Others suspect that unsubstantiated claims about cholesterol are being publicized by those, such as the manufacturers of some margarines, with an interest in non-cholesterol-containing products. You may wish to ask your doctor for advice.

Cholesterol is the most common steroid in the body. Its structural formula is:

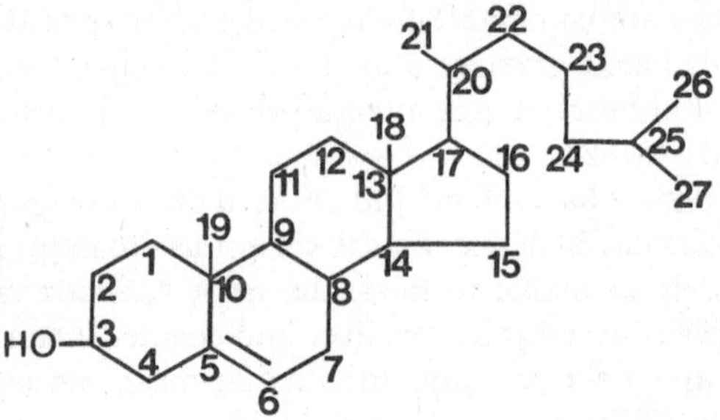

The conventional numbering of the *carbon* atoms is shown. The synthetic pathway for the formation of the molecule is interesting because in the early stages it shares the steps that plants use to synthesize rubber and vitamin A. Neither is produced by human cells.

Cholinergic

Literally, energized by choline; that is, nerve cells or neurons which release *acetylcholine* as a *transmitter* of signals between neurons, and neurons which are excited by acetylcholine. The voluntary nervous system and the parasympathetic branch of the involuntary nervous system are cholinergic. For a description of the voluntary and involuntary nervous system, see *transmitter*.

Cholinesterase (AChE)

An *enzyme* which breaks down *acetylcholine* (ACh) in the tiny synaptic gap separating nerve cells. In these *cholinergic* nerve cells, cholinesterase may also function in the process of synthesizing acetylcholine.

Certain insecticides are poisonous because they act by blocking the activity of AChE. Without the enzyme, *trans-*

mitter molecules carrying the nervous signal from one nerve cell to the next remain in the synaptic gap and at the *receptors* of post-synaptic nerve cells, abnormally prolonging the signal. Thus, a muscle cell which had been excited by a cholinergic nerve would not be allowed to return to its pre-excited state. It would be unable to respond to a new signal. The effect is a form of tetany (see also *calcium*), and a drug like atropine may be needed to block the action of the transmitter, ACh. Conversely, a disease such as myasthenia gravis reflects a condition in which too little ACh is reaching the muscle cell, for some reason. Therefore, the muscle is contracting too weakly. Such a condition may be treated with a drug like neostigmine which slows the breakdown action of cholinesterase and tends to conserve the available ACh.

Chymotrypsin

A digestive *enzyme* secreted by the pancreas into the duodenum, that portion of the intestine nearest the stomach. The enzyme splits *protein* at specific *amino acids*.

Chymotrypsin is formed from a larger molecule, chymotrypsinogen, by the action of the enzyme, *trypsin*. Chymotrypsin exists in four active forms, the differences being four amino acids. The enzyme itself catalyzes the loss of these amino acids so that in its final form, it consists of three amino-acid chains held together by two sets of two *sulphur* atoms, each set forming a disulphide bond.

Chymotrypsin and its chemical relative, trypsin, are secreted by non-islet cells in the pancreas; that is, outside the islets of Langerhans. Islet cells secrete the *hormones*, *glucagon*, *insulin* and *somatostatin*.

Citric acid

A weak *acid* with a sour taste easily extracted from lemon juice. It has the structural formula:

$$\begin{array}{c} \text{COOH} \\ | \\ \text{CH}_2 \\ | \\ \text{HOO}-\text{C}-\text{OH} \\ | \\ \text{CH}_2 \\ | \\ \text{COOH} \end{array}$$

Citric acid is found in almost all cells where it has given its name to the most important energy-producing biochemical process, the citric acid cycle, also known as the tricarboxylic acid cycle (note that citric acid contains three carboxyl (COOH) groups). Yet another name for the process is the Krebs cycle after Sir Hans Krebs, the German-born British scientist who described it and won the Nobel Prize for physiology and medicine in 1953. Inasmuch as no chemical synthesis can occur without energy to power it, the citric acid cycle is central to life. It is also central in the sense that by means of the cycle, food is utilized to make energy. With its associated processes (see below, and *cytochrome*), each cycle provides 275 Cal. for each molecular unit weight (a mole; see Appendix 2) broken down.

Each complete cycle consists of 10 chemical conversions (see Diagram). The citric acid cycle breaks down a *carbohydrate*, pyruvate, into *carbon dioxide* and water. Pyruvate is a *salt* of pyruvic acid, obtained primarily from dietary *glucose*. An acetyl group (CH_3; see Appendix 1) from pyruvate combines with a complex molecule, a *nucleotide* called coenzyme A. The product, acetyl coenzyme A, releases the acetyl group which combines with another carbohydrate, oxaloacetate, forming citrate as the first step in the cycle. Citrate is the salt of citric acid. Each transformation is catalyzed by a specific *enzyme* often with a metal *ion* as cofactor. For example, the transformation, oxalosuccinate to alpha-ketoglutarate, is catalyzed by isocitrate dehydrogenase plus manganese ion (Mn^{2+})

The breakdown of a molecular unit weight (a mole) of acetyl coenzyme A produces 215 Cal. Most of this energy is stored in *adenosine triphosphate* (ATP) formed from an ancil-

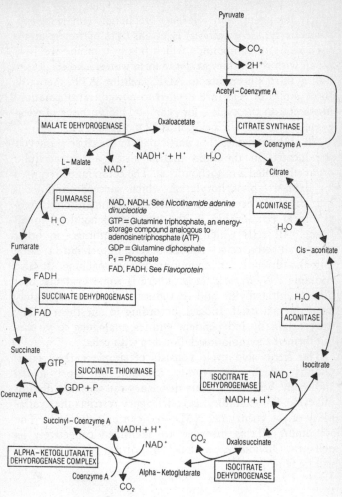

Diagram of the citric acid cycle

lary process called oxidative-phosphorylation which is made possible by the *hydrogen* ions released during the cycle and carried away by NAD and FAD (see notes in diagram). Fifteen moles of ATP are formed by the cycle, but only one appears during the cycle itself. Initially at least, that one takes the form of GTP (see notes in diagram). Oxidative-phosphorylation is not fully understood. It involves alternately taking up and releasing (reduction and oxidation, respectively; see *cytochrome*) electrons from hydrogen atoms by a series of compounds which finally combine the hydrogen with respiratory *oxygen* to form water. The effect is to link a third phosphate to ADP, creating ATP. Actually, three moles of ATP are needed to power transformations incidental to the cycle – for example, biosynthesis of coenzyme A – so that the net gain is 12 moles of ATP.

All of the enzymes that participate in the citric acid cycle are located in the fluid matrix inside an intracellular organelle called a mitochondrion. The compounds required for oxidative-phosphorylation which succeeds and feeds into the cycle occur in a suitable three-dimensional topographical relationship in the inner mitochondrial membrane. All cells which carry on biosynthesis – in other words, all active cells – contain several mitochondria. Each mitochondrion is an energy-producing machine. It also contains *deoxyribonucleic acid*. There is some evidence that mitochondria divide and reproduce themselves separately from the cell itself. Indeed, according to one theory, they were originally independent entities analogous to viruses but formed a symbiotic relationship with cells.

The citric acid cycle consists of simple carbon compounds which are readily available in most foods. Indirectly, however, dietary deficiency can seriously disrupt the cycle. For example, *niacin* deficiency restricts the availability of the coenzyme, NAD, and can halt the cycle. The symptoms of this disorder are identified collectively as pellagra. Obviously, any long-term disruption of the cycle will be fatal.

Coenzyme

A small, non-protein molecule more or less tightly linked chemically to an *enzyme* without which the enzyme cannot function. Some coenzymes are also called prosthetic groups, a phrase which implies a very tight link to the enzyme. Coenzymes are also called by the broader term, cofactor.

Some coenzymes may actually be changed by the enzymatic process. In this sense they are substrates; that is, a substance changed by an enzyme. The coenzyme is ultimately reconstituted, however, in the course of a chemical transformation in which one, if not all, of the steps is catalyzed by the original enzyme. Coenzymes cannot act as catalysts without enzymes, but they may act with a *protein* to perform a function which has physiological significance. For example, *adenosine triphosphate* (ATP) is a coenzyme in the shortening of *myosin* which underlies muscle contraction.

ATP, the energy-storage molecule, is one of the most common coenzymes. It is required to power literally hundreds of reactions, thus:

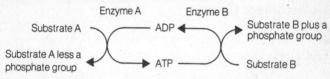

Nicotinamide adenine dinucleotide (NAD) is also a common coenzyme in energy-transfer reactions. NAD requires *niacin* for its biosynthesis. If there is a dietary deficiency of niacin, the wasting, weakness and possibly the madness of pellagra reflect the failure of cells to obtain adequate energy from other food. Other vitamins are necessary for the biosynthesis of coenzymes, as the table shows.

Vitamin	Coenzyme	Major role
Niacin(B₃)	NAD	Energy transfer
Pyridoxine (B₆) (q.v.)	Pyridoxal phosphate	Interconversion of *amino acids*
Thiamine (B₁)	Thiamine phosphate	*Carbohydrate* interconversion
B₂	Flavin adenine dinucleotide (see *citric acid, flavoprotein*)	Utilization of amino acids and carbohydrates
Folic acid	Tetrahydrofolic acid	Carbohydrate interconversion
Cyanocobalamin (B₁₂)	Corrinoids (several)	Utilization of amino acids and carbohydrates, especially for red blood cell formation
Biotin	Biotin	Skin health, growth

Perhaps the most familiar coenzyme is the haem molecule. In *haemoglobin*, the haem group transports *oxygen* and *carbon dioxide*. The same group works with various enzymes in the transfer of oxygen atoms within non-blood cells. In *cytochrome*, haem transfers electrons in the energy-storage machinery associated with the citric acid cycle. Coenzyme A, furthermore, can be looked upon as a starting point in the citric acid cycle. It is also important in the interconversion of *fats* and proteins.

Cofactor (see *Coenzyme*)

Collagen

The most common *protein* in animals, collagen is the principal constituent of connective tissue and an important element in skin, tendons, cartilage and *bone*. It consists of long protein fibres wound together in helical ropes of three. The ropes are connected by *hydrogen* bonds (see Appendix 3) to form sheets. This structure makes collagen strong and non-rigid. It is clear or yellowish in colour.

Collagen contains an unusually high quantity of the *amino acid*, hydroxyproline. One role played by vitamin C is thought to be the correct insertion of this amino acid into the protein chain. Without vitamin C, connective tissue breaks down and the symptoms of scurvy ensue.

In old age, collagen strands break and become disordered. This is one cause of the wrinkled skin and sagging tissues characteristic of age (see also *keratin*). The reason for the malformation of collagen in ageing cells is unknown. Some forms of rheumatism and certain skin diseases which reflect collagen disorders, however, are thought to be due to autoimmunity. An autoimmune disease is one in which the antigens formed by the body are attacked by *antibodies* from the same body. Many antigens are protein, and collagen is of course a protein too. Normally however, collagen is not antigenic; that is, it does not induce antibody formation even when it is transplanted into another individual providing that the two individuals are of the same species. Collagen is the same molecule in all humans, for example. If collagen disorders are caused by autoimmunity, therefore, something makes the molecule antigenic.

Copper (Cu)

(L.: *cuprum*)

A trace element required by some *enzymes* which catalyze reactions essential for growth, *blood* and *bone* formation and nerve function. Copper also plays a poorly understood role in association with *cytochrome*, a molecule required in the energy-storage process carried out by most cells.

Perhaps the best dietary source of copper is liver, but wheat germ, yeast, shellfish, curry and fruit gums contain rich supplies. Deficiency is rare but can be seen in infants fed on cow's *milk* which is low in copper. Signs of copper deficiency include anaemia, bone fractures, diarrhoea and central nervous disorders.

Inadequate copper absorption resulting in copper deficiency is caused by a rare inherited disease called Menkes syndrome. In excess, copper is a poison. Another inherited disorder, Wilson's disease, causes copper to accumulate in nerve and liver cells. Both diseases can be treated with drugs.

Copper is a reddish metal, atomic number, 29, and atomic weight, 63.54. It may act as a positive *ion* under physiological conditions.

Cortisol (see *Hydrocortisone*)

Cyanocobalamin

Vitamin B_{12}. Identified originally as a factor required to prevent a fatal blood disease, pernicious anaemia, cyanocobalamin is also essential for the formation and maintenance of the *myelin* sheath insulating the axons or long processes of many nerve cells. Deficiency of the vitamin also causes mental disturbances, dementia and spasticity.

Pernicious anaemia is a form of megaloblastic anaemia, a disorder arising from the appearance in the *bone* marrow of cells called megaloblasts. They are malformed stem cells; normal stem cells divide and give rise to the *blood* cells, erythrocytes or red blood cells, leucocytes or white cells and platelets. Megaloblastic cells fail to produce healthy blood cells.

There are other forms of anaemia arising from different conditions. If the bone marrow ceases altogether to produce blood cells, a condition called aplastic anaemia arises. In haemolytic anaemia, erythrocytes rupture because they are diseased. The chills and fever of malaria, for example, reflect an acute haemolytic anaemia caused by the emergence from red blood cells of the malarial parasite. Infections or genetic errors can cause erythrocytes to synthesize malformed *haemoglobin*. The patient is anaemic because the oxygen-transporting capacity of the blood is reduced. Thus, sickle-cell anaemia is a genetic disease which causes the synthesis of haemoglobin formed in such a way as to convert the normally flat or disc-shaped red blood cell to a sickle shape. *Iron* deficiency and of course haemorrhage may also cause anaemia. All of these conditions are serious and can be fatal. They can all be treated with reasonable hope of controlling the cause, but only cyanocobalamin can cure pernicious anaemia.

Liver is the best source of the vitamin. It is also found in meat and animal products such as *milk*, cheese and eggs. Strict vegetarians must supplement their diets with vitamin B_{12} tablets. Cyanocobalamin-deficiency can also arise because of the absence from the small intestine of a chemical, intrinsic factor, without which the vitamin cannot be absorbed. Intrinsic factor is normally produced by the stomach lining. In a few middle-aged people, synthesis stops and pernicious anaemia develops. It is thought that the cause may be an autoimmune disorder (see *antigen*). Injected vitamin B_{12} controls the condition, but it does not restore production of intrinsic factor.

Another B *vitamin, folic acid*, also plays a role in blood cell synthesis, and in the absence of cyanocobalamin, it can mask the potential anaemia. Folic acid cannot prevent the nervous degeneration caused by Vitamin B_{12} deficiency, however.

Cyanocobalamin is a complex corrinoid molecule consisting of a corrin nucleus analogous to the structure at the heart of the haem molecule in haemoglobin, but with an atom of cobalt in place of the *iron* in haem. To the cobalt are bound a cyanide molecule and a *nucleotide*. The corrin forms a *coenzyme* which acts in the interconversion of both *carbohydrates* and *amino acids*. Why the coenzyme is needed for the formation of blood cells and myelin is not understood.

Cyclic adenosine monophosphate (cAMP)

A *nucleotide* often called the 'second messenger' because in the presence of a *hormone*, the first messenger, at the cell membrane, adenosine triphosphate (ATP) is broken down to cAMP which then acts within the cell to bring about a functional change.

The breakdown of ATP is catalyzed by an *enzyme, adenyl cyclase*, thought to form a part of the cell membrane; that is, the enzyme molecule is built into the membrane structure. *Adrenaline* and *glucagon* are hormones which promote the breakdown of *glycogen* to *glucose* to be converted to energy, but the first step in the action of both hormones at their target cells is the formation of cAMP. Cyclic AMP activates another enzyme, phosphorylase kinase, which transforms yet another enzyme, phosphorylase, to a form capable of catalyzing glycogen breakdown.

Adrenocorticotropic hormone (ACTH), *luteinizing hormone* (LH) and *thyroid-stimulating hormone* (TSH) also act at the membranes of their target cells by activating adenyl cyclase. Although these hormones secreted by the pituitary gland are not directly involved in energy formation, they each stimulate synthesis of other hormones.

Cyclic AMP may enter the cell nucleus and trigger a gene that has been quiescent (see *deoxyribonucleic acid*). The activated gene would initiate biosynthesis of a new enzyme, thus altering the cell's function. The molecular machinery of this action is by no means clear, however. It is also thought that cAMP mediates the activity of some *transmitters* of signals between nerve cells. Because the transmitters are synthesized throughout the life of the cell, this role of cAMP is even less well understood.

Cyclic adenosine monophosphate is a shortened chemical name for 3'-5' adenosine monophosphate cyclic ester. An ester is an organic *salt* derived by replacing the *hydrogen* of an *acid* with an organic group, in this instance methyl, CH_2 (see Appendix 1). The structural formula is:

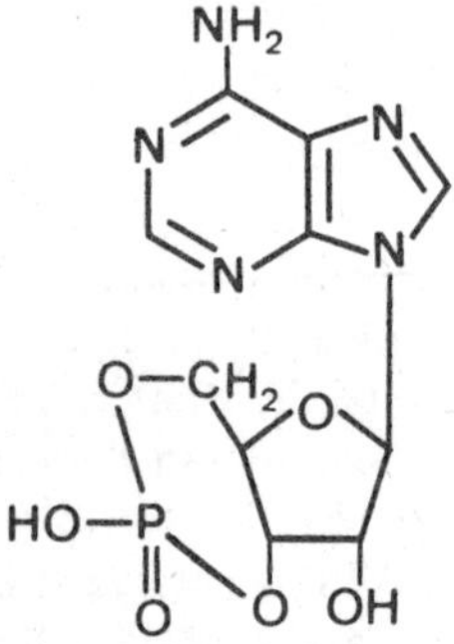

Cytochrome

One of a large class of *proteins* containing a haem group analogous to the haem in *haemoglobin* and with an atom of *iron* at its centre. There are three cytochromes in human cells. The designation, chrome, refers to the fact that, like haem, the molecule has a colour. The difference between haemoglobin and the cytochromes is in the structures of the proteins surrounding the haem.

Haemoglobin binds and transports atmospheric *oxygen*. In cytochrome, the haem also carries oxygen, but the gas is used to complete the process of energy storage begun with the breakdown of *carbohydrate* by the *citric acid* cycle. Cytochrome causes atmospheric oxygen to be changed into water. Again as with haemoglobin, once the oxygen is released, the molecule is restored to a state in which it can take up more.

Cytochromes have been found in the cells of bacteria and plants as well as all animals. There is an astonishing similarity in these proteins despite the immense variety of organisms in which they are found. Only modest differences in *amino acid* sequence occur, for example, in the cytochromes of yeast and man. This unusual molecular stability may be explained by the vital role of the haem group within the protein in the energy-storage process without which no organism can live.

That portion of the process in which the cytochromes participate is called electron transport. It is a series of oxidation-reduction steps. Oxidation requires one of three atomic changes in the molecule that is oxidized: (1) the addition of an oxygen atom, (2) the removal of a *hydrogen* atom (the first two are not necessarily alternatives but can occur almost simultaneously), and (3) the removal of one or more electrons. Reduction requires that a molecule undergoes one of the opposite events: removal of an oxygen, addition of a hydrogen or of electrons.

Oxidation can take place anaerobically; that is, in the absence of oxygen, as it does in yeast, for example, leading to fermentation. Human muscles under stress also obtain energy by the anaerobic breakdown of glucose to another carbohydrate, lactate, but this reaction produces much less energy than aerobic oxidation.

The products of the citric acid cycle include *carbon dioxide* which is taken up by the *blood* and removed, water, hydrogen *ions* (H^+) and the electrons which have been separated from H^+. The electrons are involved in a series of oxidations and reductions with the cytochromes and with flavoprotein—utilizing *nucleotides* and *nicotinamide adenine dinucleotide* (NAD). Each time NAD, for example, is oxidized by removal of an electron, it is reduced by the addition of another electron in the process called electron transport. The movement of electrons supplies the energy for oxidative phosphorylation which results in the creation of *adenosine triphosphate* (ATP), the energy-storage molecule. The precise mechanism by means of which the energy of the electrons is used to form ATP is not clear, but at the end of the process free hydrogen ions combine with atmospheric oxygen supplied by the cytochromes to form water.

Cytosine

A small molecule, one of the bases in *deoxyribonucleic acid* (DNA) and *ribonucleic acid*. Cytosine is one of a class of chemicals called pyrimidines. They can be synthesized by most cells, and they may also be obtained from food. Cytosine has the structural formula:

In the DNA double helix, the complementary base to cytosine is *quanine*.

Dentine

(L.: *dens* = tooth)

The hard outer shell of teeth, it surrounds the tooth pulp. Dentine is similar to *bone* but harder and more dense without blood vessels. It consists of organic material, largely *protein*, impregnated with lime *salts*. Tiny tubules within the mass contain processes of the cells, odontoblasts, that line the pulp cavity. The crown of the tooth dentine, above the gum, is covered by *enamel*.

Deoxyribonucleic acid (DNA)

The long, helical molecules forming the chromosomes and containing the genes. DNA is reproduced in cell division and transmitted in egg and sperm cells from parents to offspring.

Building on earlier descriptions of *protein* structure and on x-ray diffraction studies of DNA *salt* crystals, James Watson and Francis Crick proposed a model of the DNA molecule in 1953. Though modifications have had to be made in the model, its main structural hypotheses have been demonstrated experimentally. Many authorities consider the Watson–Crick model to have been the most important theoretical advance in the sciences during the twentieth century. Certainly it has given rise to a whole new field of study called molecular biology in which the structure of a molecule is used to explain or predict its function.

The Watson–Crick model emobodies:

(1) A right-handed or alpha helix. Each strand of DNA takes up the helical configuration.
(2) Two complementary strands each consisting of *nucleotides* with the four *bases*: *adenine, cytosine, guanine* and *thymine*, in varied sequences.
(3) The nucleotide *sugar* and phosphate form the outside of the helical structure so that the bases are turned inward to form links consisting of *hydrogen* bonds (see Appendix 3) with the bases of the complementary strand.

The right-handed helical structure was suggested by the description of the secondary structure of protein proposed by the American biochemist, Linus Pauling. Protein consists of *amino acids*, however, whereas DNA and other nucleic acids consist of nucleotides. Amino acids and nucleotides cannot be made to fit together in the same way because of differences in their sizes and internal atomic arrangements. In DNA, each turn of the helix consists of 10 nucleotides.

The presence in a chromosome of two complementary strands explains how the molecule functions to transmit genetic data. Before a cell divides, the strands separate, though the machinery is not understood. Each strand acts as a template for a new strand which becomes its complement. Each base will link up with only one other of the four bases: adenine with thymine, cytosine with guanine. Therefore, the presence of adenine in the template strand requires that opposite it on the new strand will be thymine. The result is an exact replication and conservation of the genetic information.

There are 46 chromosomes in human body cells, each of them consisting of two strands containing up to 100,000 nucleotides. During much of the life of the cell, excepting when the strands separate for replication, the chromosomes exist as double-stranded helixes which can be paired. Under a microscope, each chromosome in a pair looks exactly like its partner, the exception being the two sex chromosomes in a male body cell. The two female sex chromosomes are both shaped like an X, but male sex chromosomes consist of one X and one Y. That the pairs other than the sex chromosomes are chemically similar, moreover, is suggested by the fact that cells dividing to form egg or sperm cells each contain only 22 chromosomes, one strand from each pair, and one sex chromosome. To these 23 are then added at fertilization 23 from the other parent. Because male body cells contain one male and one female chromosome (each consisting of two strands), the sex of the offspring is determined by which of the father's sex chromosomes is contained in the sperm that fertilizes the egg. In any case, before the new cell divides, each chromosome again unwinds, as it were, and replication occurs as in any other body cell.

Much of the machinery of replication is poorly understood. What does seem clear is that the sequence of bases on each strand spells out the individual inheritance in a genetic alphabet of four letters: A for adenine, C for cytosine, G for guanine and T for thymine. To understand how that alphabet of bases functions, it is necessary to explain more fully the chemical role of DNA. Not only does each strand act as a template for new DNA, but also during the life of the cell, each strand forms a template for another, related chemical, *ribonucleic acid* (RNA). (In fact, only one chromosome in a pair or indeed one strand in one chromosome per pair – i.e., ¼ of a pair – may act as a template for the formation of RNA.) RNA itself is then translated into protein. Protein consists of amino acids linked together in a long chain. However, there are only four bases in DNA and RNA, but proteins consist of some 20 amino acids. The genetic alphabet of four letters must somehow be made to identify one of 20 alternatives. Clearly, the four-base alphabet must be doubled up in some way.

The everyday English alphabet consists of 26 letters which are combined to form millions of words in a similar manner. Thus, instead of 1 = 1, 2 = 2 and so on, each genetic 'word', or codon, consists of three bases. Doubling alone gives only 16 'words', not enough. The three-base words can be represented: AAA, AAC, ACA, CAA, CAC, CCC, AAG, AGA, GAA, GAG and so on through a total of 64 combinations. Thus, GAC is transcribed into RNA and the RNA bases are translated into the amino acid, leucine. Similarly, CCC is translated via RNA to *glycine*. With 64 possible codons in the genetic code, more than one can mean one amino acid, though. Some of the codons appear to be silent; that is, they are not translated but have some other functions. For example, some convey instructions like 'start here' or 'stop here'.

Two interesting questions about the function of DNA remain unanswered. The first is: how are the strands actually unwound and made available for transcription? The second is really a special case of the first: how is transcription initiated?

Unwinding requires the catalytic action of *enzymes*, but the course of events is unclear. Along each strand of DNA about 1,500 bases on average form a gene. There appear to be silent base sequences separating the genes and occasionally splitting them, but each gene sequence with its initiator and concluding three-base codons is translated via RNA into protein. In other words, the manner in which the chromosome expresses itself in the structure and function of a cell is in the form of proteins. Now, obviously not all cells have the same structures or functions. Skin cells, for example, neither look nor act like nerve cells. Yet all body cells have exactly the same chromosomes and, therefore, the same genes. Some are transcribed and translated in some cells but not in others. Put differently, some genes are suppressed in all cells. The machinery operating this vital selectivity is not understood.

An especially acute aspect of the initiation problem is

seen in cancer cells. These diseased cells escape the limits normally imposed on cell division. It is thought that the disorder reflects a change in the DNA, a mutation, which alters its chemistry in some subtle fashion. Broadly speaking, mutations are of two kinds. Point mutations involve the deletion or addition of a nucleotide in the chain. Such a change alters the codon sequence, and a new protein is eventually synthesized, implying a change in the structure and function of the cell.

It is also now known that whole sequences of nucleotides may be removed, added in or displaced within the chain. On the whole, the evidence suggests that it is this kind of mutation rather than point mutation which underlies cancer.

Many accidents can cause mutations. Ionizing radiation such as cosmic rays or the fallout from a nuclear explosion produces point mutations. Many chemicals and drugs can also damage DNA by nucleotide deletion or displacement. Some viruses consist of DNA which may be inserted into the DNA of an infected cell. In bacteria, resistance to antibiotics can be transferred from one bacterium to another by means of a piece of the DNA from the resistant organism, but it is not clear that analogous transfers can occur between human cells.

According to the accepted laws of Darwinian evolution, those members of a species that are best adapted to an environment will survive and produce offspring. Most mutations either have no effect, or they are damaging to the individual as in cases where they lead to cancer, but a few may improve the adaptability of that individual and those of its offspring which inherit the mutated gene. In theory at least, structural or functional changes acquired by an individual as a result of its adaptation to the environment are not incorporated into the DNA and therefore cannot be transmitted to offspring. Thus, it is wrong to assume, for example, that dark skin colour caused by tanning in bright sunlight is passed on to children. Rather, the individuals whose skin happens to be tinted with a bit more *melanin* suffer less skin cancer, let us say, in tropical sunshine than individuals with less melanin and lighter coloured skin. In the tropics a dark skin contributes to relatively longer life with a consequent enhancement of the opportunity to produce children.

In the decades since the discovery of the DNA structure in 1953, however, two types of evidence have tended to contradict the accepted theory. Perhaps the first was the discovery that some viruses containing RNA instead of DNA could cause sequence mutations like those following DNA-virus infection. According to Crick and Watson, DNA acts as a template for RNA and not the other way round. The discovery in all body cells, however, of an enzyme, reverse transcriptase, has been followed by the demonstration that DNA can be transcribed from RNA. There is still no evidence, though, that protein can act as a template for RNA or DNA in cells, and thus no direct evidence that acquired characteristics might be inherited.

The second indication that this is, nevertheless, possible is the transfer of antibiotic resistance by means of the exchange of bits of DNA. Resistance thus acquired is indeed transmitted to subsequent generations of bacteria and looks very much like inheritance of a trait acquired at least in part in response to environmental pressure. Until the laws governing transcription are better understood, theories contradicting Darwinian principles of inheritance must remain suspect.

The chromosomes are found in the cell nucleus, but DNA also occurs in another cellular organelle, the mitochondrion. Many tiny, multi-folded mitochondria are found in most cells. Their principal function is the breakdown of *carbohydrates* to obtain energy (see *citric acid*, *cytochrome*). The role of DNA in mitochondria is not clear, but according to one theory, the organelles originated as independent entities which colonized or parasitized cells successfully because of the symbiotic relationship which developed between them.

Dopa

A small molecule synthesized from the *amino acid*, tyrosine.

Dopa is a precursor of *dopamine* and *noradrenaline*, both of which are *transmitters* of signals between nerve cells.

Dopa can be administered as a drug by injection and will enter the brain whereas its product, dopamine, will not. Since the discovery that the movement disorder, Parkinson's disease, is associated with abnormal depletion of dopamine in part of the brain, dopa has been used to control Parkinsonian symptoms. Like many other organic molecules, however, dopa has two forms: in crystals, one form diffracts polarized light to the right and is called dextrodopa (D-dopa). The other diffracts polarized light to the left, laevo-dopa (L-dopa). In life, most birefringent molecules occur in the L but not the D form. Probably for this reason, dopa consisting of a mixture of the two forms proved to be an unsatisfactory drug, and only L-dopa is used. Unfortunately, it is not a cure for Parkinson's disease. Because the unknown causes of the disease continue to operate, L-dopa eventually ceases to provide even symptomatic relief.

Dopa is a *catecholamine* with the structural formula:

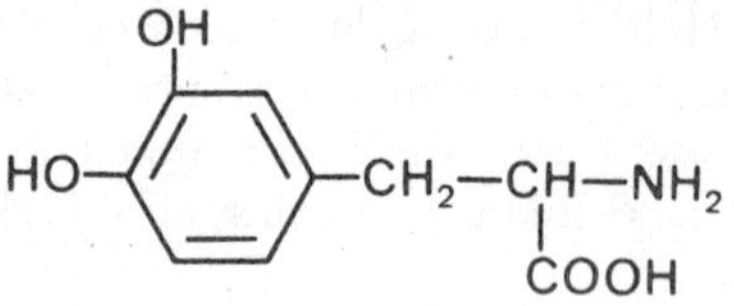

Dopamine

A small molecule which acts as a *transmitter* of signals between many nerve cells in the basal ganglia, a part of the brain which relays movement orders from the cortex to the muscles, and possibly also information about the location of the limbs back to the cortex. Abnormal depletion of dopamine in the basal ganglia accompanies the movement disorder, Parkinson's disease, but the cause of the depletion is not known.

Dopamine is an excitatory transmitter; that is, it stimulates a nerve cell to send a signal. Other transmitters are inhibitory; they tend to delay signalling by a nerve cell.

Dopamine is the precursor of *noradrenaline* and is synthesized from *dopa*. Like these two substances, it is a *catecholamine* with the structural formula:

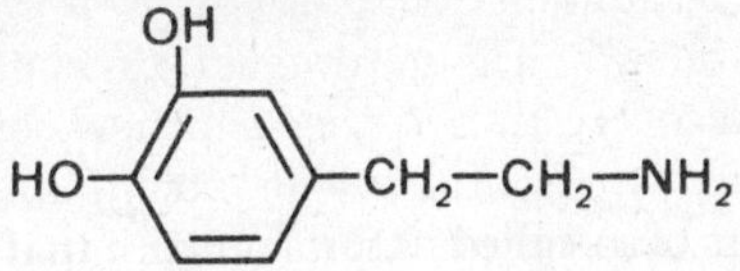

Electrolyte

A compound which will conduct an electric current when it is in solution. Whereas in solids an electric current consists of electrons, the current flowing through an electrolytic solution is conducted by *ions* into which the electrolyte is dissociated. For example, ordinary table salt (NaCl) dissociates in solution to form Na^+ and Cl^-. Both are ions, *sodium* a positive ion and *chlorine*, negative, as indicated. Salt, therefore, is an electrolyte.

In medicine, the word is used more loosely to include the two ions. Incidentally, many electrolytes will also conduct electric current when in a molten state, a condition which is not relevant to most organisms.

Enamel

The hard, white *mineral* substance covering the crown of the *dentine*. Dentine makes up the bulk of the tooth. Like *bone* and dentine, enamel also consists principally of *calcium* and *phosphorus* in the form of phosphate. Its organic matrix is *keratin*, and it is the hardest organic substance known.

Enamel is laid down by special superficial cells in the mouth and gum. The absence of vitamin A during prenatal life or infancy can cause a degeneration of these enamelling cells leading to the production of defective enamel. A high calcium diet is also imperative during the time of tooth-formation, but after they have erupted, neither high calcium nor vitamin A dietary content can reduce decay. Traces of vanadium, molybdenum, selenium and fluorine in drinking water may strengthen tooth enamel, but many people believe that there is an hereditary element in tooth decay causing some of us to have more resistant tooth enamel than others.

Endorphin

One of a class of so-called natural opiates; that is, chemicals found in body cells especially in parts of the brain and spinal cord which act like morphine and other drugs derived from opium or synthetic chemicals with a similar structure. Endorphin is a *peptide* consisting of a short chain of *amino acids*. The most fully described opioid peptides are alpha* and beta endorphin and leucine – and methionine-enkephalin. All natural opiates are found in many other mammals beside humans.

The discovery of the opioid peptides affords an unusual insight into modern biological research. For centuries, men have used the juice of the opium poppy, *Papaver somniferum*, as a narcotic and analgesic; that is, a drug that produces sleep and relief from pain. That opium is also a drug of addiction has been recognized from the time of its earliest use.

In 1803, a German chemist named Sertürner purified the most active ingredient of the poppy juice and called it morphine. Codeine is also a natural derivative of opium. It is much less powerful than morphine, but like all natural and synthetic opium-like chemicals before the endorphins, it too is addictive. Heroin is a semi-synthetic opiate; methadone, wholly synthetic. None of these chemicals is found in humans or other animals.

The question raised by the opiates and many other drugs (see also *tranquillizer, natural*) is how they cause beneficial changes in human and other animal cells. To answer it, the *receptor* theory of chemical interactions with cells was advanced in the early part of this century by the German physiologist, Paul Ehrlich. According to the theory, any chemical that alters the behaviour of a cell must first become attached to specialized molecules or receptors in the cell membrane. Receptors are believed to exist for

*See end of entry.

antibodies, antigens, hormones and *transmitters* as well as foreign chemicals.

Although many drugs like the opiates are found in nature, they are not found in animals. Logically, however, a receptor for a drug must also be the receptor for a naturally occurring chemical. Otherwise how would the receptor molecule have appeared in the cell membrane? The Darwinian theory of evolution holds that any characteristic reflects the body's physical adjustment. Therefore, a receptor for an opiate must also be a receptor for some substance within the body.

Because morphine is both valuable as a pain killer and seriously addictive, the search began a generation ago for a natural opiate capable of analgesia without addiction. An opiate receptor was indeed identified, and then in 1975, Dr John Hughes and his colleagues at the University of Aberdeen isolated from animal brain extract two peptides which had effects analogous to those of the opiates when they were injected into other animals. They found by analysis of the chemicals that both consisted of five amino acids, differing in that the fifth amino acid counted from the end of the molecule containing a carboxyl (COOH) group was methionine in one and in the other, leucine. Hughes and his associates named the molecules enkephalins. It appeared that the natural opiates had been found.

Almost inevitably, the truth is far more complex. Hope was soon dashed that the enkephalins might serve as powerful new drugs that could mimic the analgesic effect of morphine without its addictive effect. Enkephalin acts like an antigen when it is used as a drug, arousing allergy-like reactions against it. There is no allergic response to morphine because the drug molecule is not a peptide and does not act like an antigen.

At the beginning of the 1980s, synthetic chemicals similar to enkephalin were being tested as analgesics. Other chemicals which act by inhibiting the activity of *enzymes* catalyzing the breakdown of enkephalin may extend the life of the opioid peptides and thus increase the effectiveness of the substances already in the body. Research has also been directed towards stimulation of secretion of the naturally occurring chemicals. In 1981, for example, the British Medical Association approved research into the use of electrical stimulation which increases the blood level of endorphins to control the symptoms of withdrawal from opiate addiction. This work originated in mounting evidence that analgesia obtained either by acupuncture or by superficial electrical stimulation is produced by elevated blood levels of the opioid peptides.

These fascinating chemicals may eventually have another therapeutic use. In one study, one type of endorphin dramatically relieved the symptoms of chronic schizophrenia in a group of patients. This gamma-endorphin is not an analgesic though it differs in only one amino acid from the endorphins that do act like opiates.

Research into the opioid peptides has naturally continued. A larger peptide molecule was identified, consisting of 31 amino acids. It includes the five amino-acid sequence of methionine enkephalin, and is now known as beta-endorphin. Another molecule with only 17 amino acids contains the five-amino acid sequence of leucine enkephalin and has been named alpha-endorphin.* The two endorphins appeared to be the natural precursors of the enkephalins. They also have analgesic qualities, but being peptides, they too are antigenic.

It is now believed that the enkephalins are synthesized from the endorphins, but that both substances – or rather, all four – may originate from some other large molecule. There is evidence that *adrenocorticotropic hormone* (ACTH) and *growth hormone*, both peptide molecules, also originate in a large molecule, and that it is the same molecule that gives rise to the endorphins. Like the two hormones, moreover, the endorphins may be secreted by the pituitary gland beneath the brain in the bony roof of the mouth. The enkephalins may originate in another part of the brain altogether. Indeed, different nerve cells are thought to secrete each of the two enkephalins. They are also secreted by the adrenal medulla, the central portion of the adrenal glands on top of the kidneys. All of the opioid peptides are found in the *cerebrospinal fluid* and in the *blood*.

In the brain, enkephalin could affect transmission of

signals between nerve cells or neurons. If it does, it probably inhibits neùrons from releasing *transmitter*. Thus, enkephalin may inhibit the signalling of pain messages from the periphery to the cortex.

* Now called dynorphin. Alpha-Neo endorphin is a slightly smaller peptide molecule.

Enkephalin (see *Endorphin*)

Enzyme

(Gr.: *en* = in + *zyme* = leaven)

A protein molecule often including a non-protein *coenzyme* which facilitates or catalyzes chemical changes that would otherwise take place more slowly under biological conditions. For example, *carbon* compounds can be broken down to *carbon dioxide* and water with the release of energy very rapidly by burning. In the body, this breakdown is accomplished with about the same speed. Although some heat is generated, much more of the energy is conserved (see *citric acid*). The slow breakdown of carbon compounds which takes place outside the body at 37 degrees Centigrade, body temperature, in the presence of *oxygen* and water would be completely inconsistent with the need for rapid movement such as speech or a defensive reflex action. Only the presence of enzymes permits the existence of life as we experience it.

The word, enzyme, was coined because the first to be recognized were those in yeast which contribute to the reverse process, the release of oxygen which can be used to leaven bread. Literally thousands of enzymes have now been identified as distinctive proteins performing a vast range of functions, and the list is by no means complete. Many enzyme structures have been analysed in detail, and a few have even been synthesized in laboratories.

These vital molecules share three important characteristics. They are catalysts; that is, they participate in and facilitate chemical changes but emerge themselves unchanged. They are large proteins consisting of several hundred *amino acids*. Thirdly, because each one has a unique amino-acid sequence, every enzyme has a distinctive conformation (see *protein* for a general description) which determines its chemical specificity.

By and large one enzyme performs one catalytic function; that is, it facilitates only one or a very small number of closely related chemical changes. For example, there are two digestive enzymes, *chymotrypsin* and *trypsin*, synthesized in the pancreas and secreted into the intestine where they help to break down protein. As the diagram shows, chymotrypsin breaks only one bond between an aromatic amino acid (one containing a benzene ring, see Appendix 1) and any other amino acid. Trypsin breaks only one bond between the amino acids, lysine or arginine, and any other amino acid.

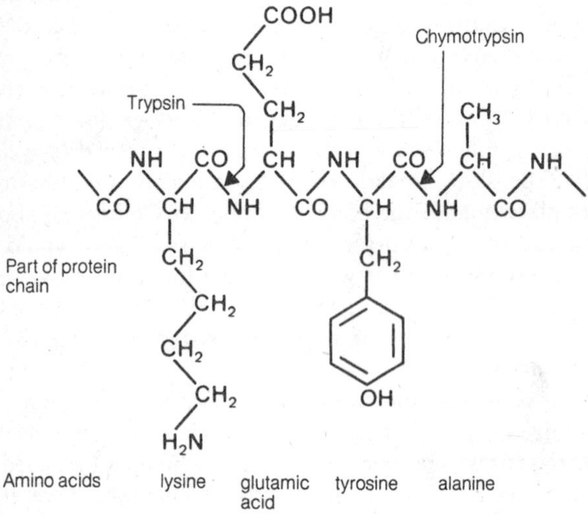

This specificity is the result of chemical forces within the molecule produced by the amino-acid sequence. At least two of the amino acids, probably widely separated from each other in the chain, are brought close together by the conformation of the molecule to form what is called an active site:

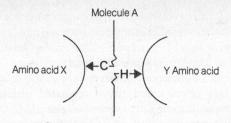

Molecule A

Amino acid X ← C / H → Y Amino acid

Molecule A is called the substrate. Amino acids X and Y are part of the enzyme. The substrate is attracted by chemical forces to the enzyme molecule in such a way that part of molecule A is threaded into the active site. There, a chemical reaction occurs. In the diagram, two atoms, *carbon* (C) and *hydrogen* (H), in molecule A are more strongly attracted to the amino acids X and Y, respectively, than to each other, and molecule A is broken. The two fragments of molecule A having changed their own atomic relationships and topography are now released and the enzyme is ready to catalyze the breakdown of another molecule A.

The coenzyme, if there is one, may play the role of moving the extra atoms away from the active site. For example, one function of *nicotinamide adenosine dinucleotide* is to carry away extra hydrogen. In some enzymes, the coenzyme provides energy for the catalytic action, or it may collect energy released during the process. For other actions, see *Coenzyme*.

Enzyme specificity is a function of the protein structure. It is this structure which is determined by the genes inherited by the individual (see *deoxyribonucleic acid, ribonucleic acid*). Thus, it is principally the enzymes which give genes effect in cells, although some genes direct the synthesis of structural protein such as *keratin* and proteins involved in transport including *cytochrome* and *haemoglobin*. Enzymes are one important means by which genetic differences are given phenotypic or outward physical manifestation. Similarly, though all body cells in one individual contain the same genes, not all body cells look and act in the same way. The cells forming the cornea of the eyeball, for example, differ profoundly from a nerve cell. This difference is also expressed in the first instance by the proteins produced in the respective cells, especially the enzymes. Why different cells in the same body synthesize different enzymes, or in other words why gene expression differs from one cell to another, is not understood.

There is information, however, about the related question of how enzyme quantity is regulated within the cell. For example, the enzyme, *monoamine oxidase* (MAO), catalyzes synthesis and breakdown of certain *transmitters* of nerve signals between nerve cells. If these cells have been very active, more enzyme molecules may be needed not just because more signals are being sent but also because all organic molecules 'wear out' eventually and have to be replaced. The monoamine-oxidase gene must be activated. Cells do not contain unlimited resources, moreover, and the amino acids needed to synthesize monoamine oxidase may be needed elsewhere. One or two are transmitters themselves, for example (see *glycine*). Finally, when it is no longer needed, the MAO gene must be turned off. This regulation may be performed by the enzyme itself. The correct number of enzyme molecules appears to be preset by some unknown mechanism. Any variation switches the gene on or off.

Like drugs, *hormones* and many other chemicals, enzymes have both a systematic and a trivial name. The former describes the chemical nature and exact location in the substrate molecule of the transformation catalyzed by the enzyme. Thus, trypsin is the trivial name for 3,4,4,4 peptide peptidohydrolase.

Most enzymes are now identified by the suffix,—ase. A few, principally the digestive enzymes like trypsin and *pepsin*, retain the trivial names given to them when they were described before the variety and universality of enzymes had been appreciated.

Enzymes are classified by their chemical function: oxidoreductases (see *cytochrome*), transferases (catalyzing transfers of a group of atoms, especially amino acids, from one substrate to another), hydrolases (catalyzing breakdowns that require water), ligases (catalyzing the combining of two molecules and requiring energy obtained from a coenzyme such as *adenosine triphosphate*), lyases (catalyzing breaking or forming certain specific bonds) and isomerases (which cause a molecule to change its internal structure and therefore its properties).

The Commission on Enzymes of the International Union of Biochemistry maintains an up-to-date list of enzymes, but it is neither necessary nor indeed possible within the space available to offer anything like a complete catalogue of known body enzymes. The following are enzymes described by entries in the *Dictionary*, or they are named in the entries specified. Their general physiological functions are listed but not their biochemical classifications. Only trivial names are used:

Enzyme	Entry (if not separately defined)	Function
Aconitase	*Citric acid*	Energy formation
Adenyl cyclase		Energy transduction
Alcohol dehydrogenase		Detoxification
Alpha-ketoglutarate dehydrogenase	*Citric acid*	Energy formation
Amylase		Starch digestion
Carbonic anhydrase	*Carbonic acid*	*Electrolyte* balance
Carboxypeptidase		Protein digestion
Cholinesterase		Nervous activity
Chymotrypsin		Protein digestion
Citrate synthetase	*Citric acid*	Energy formation
Erepsin	*Pepsin*	Protein digestion
Fumarase	*Citric acid*	Energy formation
Galactose uridyl transferase	*Galactose*	*Sugar* digestion
Glutamic acid decarboxylase	*Gamma-amino butyric acid*	Nervous activity
Hyaluronidase	*Hyaluronic acid*	Tissue integrity
Isocitrate dehydrogenase	*Citric acid*	Energy formation
Lactase	*Lactose*	Sugar digestion
Lipase		*Fat* digestion
Lyzozyme (neuraminidase)		*Antigen* destruction
Malate dehydrogenase	*Citric acid*	Energy formation
Monoamine oxidase		Nervous activity
O-diphenol oxidase	*Melanin*	Pigmentation
Pepsin		Protein digestion
Phosphoglucomutase	*Glucose*	Energy transduction
Phosphorylase	*Adrenaline, adrenocorticotropic hormone, cyclic-adenosine monophosphate, glucose*	Energy transduction

Enzyme	Entry (if not separately defined)	Function
Phosphorylase kinase	*Cyclic-adenosine monophosphate*	Energy transduction
Ptyalin	*Amylase, saliva*	Starch digestion
Renin		Electrolyte balance
Reverse transcriptase	*Deoxyribonucleic acid, interferon*	DNA synthesis from ribonucleic acid template
Succinate dehydrogenase	*Citric acid*	Energy formation
Succinate thiokinase	*Citric acid*	Energy formation
Trypsin		Protein digestion

Epinephrine (see *Adrenaline*)

Erepsin (see *Pepsin*)

Erythropoietin

A *hormone* secreted by the kidneys in response to inadequate *oxygen* intake which causes red blood cells to be formed by the *bone* marrow. *Androgens*, the male hormones, stimulate erythropoietin synthesis, a fact which may explain the higher red cell count in males.

Red blood cells or erythrocytes evolve in bone marrow from a relatively undifferentiated stem cell. Alternatively, the stem cell can develop into any one of the formed elements of the *blood*. It does so by cell division and other processes, but the mechanism by means of which its line of descent is determined is not understood. Erythropoietin acts to stimulate the formation of erythrocytes rather than white cells or platelets.

It is formed in the kidneys from a precursor, erythrogenin, by the action of a *blood factor* synthesized in the liver. The hormone is a *protein* combined with a *carbohydrate* and displays chemical similarities to another blood factor, α_2 *globulin*.

Faeces (see *Bile*)

Fat

One of the three main constituents of organic matter along
with *carbohydrate* and *protein* and therefore a constituent of
food. However, fruits, many vegetables, coffee and tea
contain very little fat or none at all. Apart from the
separated fats – butter, cream, lard, oils – the best sources
are peanuts, streaky bacon, chocolate, cheddar cheese, pork
loin, plain biscuits, herring, roast beef and eggs, in that
order!

Fat provides more energy per unit weight than any other
nutrient. Each gram of fat supplies about 9 kCal whereas a
gram of carbohydrate or protein produces less than half
that amount. Excepting for one fat constituent, linoleic acid
(see *lipid*), the liver can synthesize all fats from protein and
carbohydrate. To obtain the energy supplied by relatively
small amounts of fat, however, the diet must be much more
bulky.

A bulky diet is thought to have advantages related to the
more rapid movement of nutrients and waste through the
intestines. On the other hand, a fat-free diet is unwise for
normal people. At least three *vitamins*, A, D and E, are fat
soluble and must be taken as supplements if they are not
obtained through a diet containing some fat. The absorption of fats is also related to the intake of *folic acid* and
vitamin B_{12} (*cyanocobalamin*; see also *bile*). Fat has another
dietary advantage, moreover: it can be eaten almost pure
whereas water is usually needed to make carbohydrates
edible.

Yet there is statistical evidence that excessive fat intake is
related to heart and circulatory disease. The unsaturated
fats obtained from vegetable oils are thought to be less
conducive to heart disease than the saturated fats in animal
products such as butter (for the chemical differences
between saturated and unsaturated fats, see *lipid*).
Although the medical profession in the United States has
tended to accept this as an indication that animal fats cause

heart disease, the British Medical Association has not. (See also, *cholesterol*.) Quite apart from cardiovascular disorders, however, less serious conditions such as gout are also associated with excessive fat intake.

At body temperature, fats have the consistency of oil. Fats and oils are merely different forms of the same substance, but mineral oils obtained, for example, from petroleum are not fats. They are different chemicals entirely.

Fat plays many functional roles in the body apart from supplying energy. It may be converted into *cholestorol*, *hormones* and *steroids*. Fat molecules are the principal constituents of cell membranes where they are often combined with carbohydrates to form glycolipids. *Myelin*, the sheath surrounding many nerve cell processes, is a fat.

When it is not being used, fat is stored in layers throughout the body. In this form, it serves as insulation and as a cushion against external pressure, for example, for the delicate lactatory glands of the breasts. When the fat layer or adipose tissue lies just beneath the skin as it does over the gut, for example, it can be surgically removed, an operation sometimes carried out to reduce the strain on the heart imposed by the extra capillary length needed to service the fat layers and by the extra body weight. Fat is stored in fat cells; thus, fat layers consist of cells in the same way as muscle or nervous tissue. The stored fat consists of tiny droplets within the fat cells.

Fat is stored either as white or as brown adipose tissue. The white is more common. It is made up of cells containing relatively few droplets of a colourless fat. In young animals including humans, about half of the fat store is brown adipose tissue made up of cells containing many more droplets. Brown fat is found especially across the upper chest and back, and it is now also believed to occur in normal human adults. Indeed, there is evidence for a theory that obesity, a disease in which the body becomes grossly overweight for whatever reason, is associated with a deficiency of brown fat. Brown fat is converted to energy more rapidly than white though the reason for this is not clear. There is also evidence that brown-fat conversion is regulated by nervous centres in the hypothalamus, a part of the mid-brain which controls the body's response to temperature changes. In young animals whose temperature control machinery is still immature, the first response to temperature change, especially cooling, is rapid conversion of brown fat to heat energy. Some adults may lack normal brown-fat deposits, perhaps because of an inherited disease. Without this source of rapid heat energy, their bodies may respond more slowly to temperature shifts. Again, cooling would be the most critical problem because, if the body temperature is less responsive, chemical processes or metabolism are slowed. White adipose tissue then tends to accumulate. It is an important theory, but one which lacks proof as yet.

In accordance with the British practice, the biochemistry of fat and of the energy it supplies will be described under *lipid*.

Fatty acid (see *Lipid*)

Fibrin (see *Blood factor*)

Flavoprotein

A class of *enzymes* in which there is a *coenzyme* containing *riboflavin, vitamin* B_2.

In some flavoproteins, the coenzyme also contains a metal atom, usually *iron*. All flavoproteins catalyze oxidation-reduction reactions (see *cytochrome*); that is, they remove or add an electron either from or to the substrate or from or to another coenzyme, nicotinamide adenine dinucleotide phosphate (NADP; see *nicotinamide adenine dinucleotide*). For example, the transaction with NADP occurs as part of the process concluding the energy-releasing breakdown of *glucose* which is initiated in the *citric acid* cycle.

In flavoproteins, the riboflavin coenzyme is either combined with a *sugar* only as in flavin mononucleotide, or with a sugar and the *base, adenine,* as in flavin adenine dinuc-leotide (FAD). The coenzyme, FAD, contains two phosphate groups and provides energy from the breaking of the second phosphate bond for the transformations catalyzed by the enzyme.

Fluid (see *Blood, Body fluid, Cerebrospinal fluid, Lymph, Saliva, Semen, Sweat, Vitreous humour*)

Folic acid

One of the B *vitamins* but customarily unnumbered. Folic acid deficiency produces serious anaemia similar to the pernicious anaemia caused by *cyanocobalamin* (vitamin B_{12})-deficiency.

The best sources of folic acid are liver and dark green vegetables such as spinach, broccoli, spring greens and watercress. However, even relatively poor sources such as meat, fish and milk usually supply enough of the vitamin for the normal person. Curiously, bacteria which inhabit the large intestine produce free folic acid, but it is of no use to us because absorption takes place through the walls of the small intestine. The liver stores three to four months' supply of folic acid in most people, but pregnant women may well use up their reserves. Unless they take supplementary doses, they become anaemic with a risk to themselves as well as to the foetus. Infants whose livers are not yet fully matured may also suffer anaemia caused by folic acid deficiency.

Like pernicious anaemia, this disorder reflects the development in *bone* marrow of deformed stem cells called megaloblasts. Normal stem cells evolve into the formed elements of the *blood*, red and white cells and platelets. Megaloblasts cannot divide. Folic acid plays a fundamental role in the growth and reproduction of cells. In bone marrow, it is thought to act before cyanocobalamin in the vital processes that produce healthy stem cells. Folic acid is essential in the formation of the nucleic acids (see *deoxyribo-*

nucleic acid, ribonucleic acid) and of the *amino acids, glycine* and serine. It plays an indirect role in the biosynthesis of these cellular constituents.

Administered folic acid can correct uncomplicated mega-loblastic anaemia, but if a vitamin B_{12}-deficiency is also present causing classical pernicious anaemia, folic acid cannot help. The nervous disorder caused by B_{12}-deficiency, moreover, is never cured by folic acid.

The vitamin must be activated in the body, a process which consists of its conversion to a closely related chemical, folinic acid (or tetrahydrofolic acid). Activation can only take place in the presence of another vitamin, *ascorbic acid* (vitamin C). The activated molecule differs from folic acid because of the addition of a formyl (CHO) group, encircled by a dotted line in the structural formula, and of four hydrogen atoms to the rings on the left:

p-amino-benzoic acid   glutamic acid

The p-amino-benzoic acid segment (p = para; that is, a benzene ring (see Appendix 1) with the substitution for two *hydrogen* atoms of two atoms linked to opposite *carbon* atoms) is similar to sulphanilamide, one of the earliest antibacterial drugs. It kills or slows the development of bacteria because it interferes with their ability to synthesize folic acid. In other words, after treatment with sulphanilamide, bacteria which normally synthesize their own folic acid must have it as a vitamin, but unlike humans who can absorb preformed folic acid, the bacteria cannot.

Follicle-stimulating hormone (FSH)

One of the *hormones* which regulates the monthly oestral cycle in women. In men, it stimulates testicular growth and the early phases of sperm development.

Follicles are the egg-bearing sacks in the uterus. The

hormone is secreted by the forward or anterior portion of the pituitary gland beneath the mid-brain in the bony roof of the mouth. The hypothalamus, a brain centre directly above and connected to the pituitary, secretes an FSH-*releasing factor* in response to a fall in the *blood* level of the female hormone, *oestrogen*. The trigger in men is less clear. FSH is secreted during the first two weeks of the oestral cycle causing the egg in the ovarian follicle to 'ripen'. Normally, only one follicle at a time is affected. At mid-cycle, the follicle begins to secrete large amounts of oestrogen, shutting down the output of FSH-releasing factor and of FSH.

In men, the hormone may be secreted as an accessory to interstitial-cell-stimulating hormone (ICSH; see *luteinizing hormone*) which is also required for the production of sperm. Like FSH, ICSH is secreted by the anterior pituitary along with another hormone, prolactin. All three are classified as gonadotropic hormones because they stimulate the gonads or reproductive organs. Human chorionic gonadotropin, a fourth member of this class, is produced by the placenta.

After menopause the ovary no longer produces oestrogen. High blood levels of FSH can occur causing the post-menopausal hot flushes. This uncomfortable disorder can be controlled by contraceptive pills containing oestrogen.

Drugs chemically related to FSH are used in conjunction with the other gonadotropins to overcome female sterility by stimulating the ovary to produce an egg. There is no evidence that they have helped to correct male sterility.

FSH is a glycoprotein; that is, a molecule consisting of a *protein* bound to a *carbohydrate*. Like many other hormones it acts by binding to cellular receptors stimulating the *enzyme, adenyl cyclase*, to convert *adenosine triphosphate* to *cyclic-adenosine monophosphate*.

Fructose

Fruit *sugar* obtained naturally from honey, apples, pears and some other fruits. Fructose may also be called laevulose.

Fructose is a *carbohydrate* like all sugars. It is a simple sugar or monosaccharide consisting of only one *carbon* ring. In sucrose or ordinary white sugar, a disaccharide, fructose is combined with *glucose*. In the liver, fructose can also be converted to glucose.

In sucrose, the fructose molecule consists of a five-membered ring:

Fructose may also exist in the form of a six-membered ring like glucose.

Galactose

A simple *sugar* or monosaccharide obtained principally from *milk* and milk products. In milk, galactose occurs in combination with *glucose* as *lactose*, a disaccharide. Galactose may also be obtained from offal.

In the liver, galactose is converted to glucose. A small number of children suffer from a disease called galactosaemia; that is, they have an excess of galactose in their *blood* because they cannot convert it to glucose. The disease is caused by a genetic error in which a gene is either missing or malformed (see *deoxyribonucleic acid*). Because of the error an *enzyme*, galactose uridyl transferase, is either missing or malformed. Galactose and another compound, galactose-6-phosphate, accumulate in the blood causing blindness, mental retardation and liver damage. The toxic effects of galactosaemia can be avoided by rigid exclusion of galactose-containing foods including milk from the diet. Infants are now usually screened at birth for this disorder and for an analogous genetic error affecting the utilization of an *amino acid*, phenylalanine. In Britain, about 1 in 70,000 children suffer from galactosaemia. The genetic error is usually inherited, but it can occur as a mutation in the individual.

Like all sugars, galactose is a *carbohydrate*. The molecule consists of a six-membered ring:

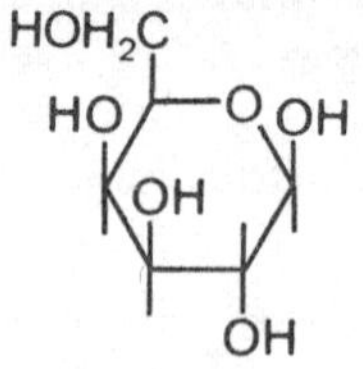

Gamma-amino butyric acid (GABA)

A small *amino-acid* molecule, one of the chemical *transmitters* of signals between nerve cells or neurons in the brain. GABA is secreted by neurons in the basal ganglia and the limbic system, two clusters of cells in the mid-brain. The basal ganglia relay movement orders from the cortex to the muscles and information about the location of the limbs to the cortex. The limbic system plays a role in the emotions and in alertness. GABA is an inhibitory transmitter, one which acts to reduce the likelihood that a signal will appear in a neuron.

Abnormal depletion of GABA or its malfunction is associated with severe movement disorders such as Huntington's chorea, a fatal disease which may also produce dementia. Whether the GABA malfunction also underlies the dementia is not clear. Some authorities argue that GABA is a natural anti-convulsant; that is, a substance that prevents excessive and uncoordinated muscular contractions. They suggest that some GABA-related malfunction may also underlie epilepsy, but no direct evidence in support of this theory has yet been found.

The causes of both Huntington's chorea and epilepsy are probably extremely complex, and so far, research into the biochemistry of GABA has revealed only interesting suggestions. GABA is synthesized in neurons and in other cells from another amino acid, glutamic acid, with the catalytic assistance of an *enzyme*, glutamic acid decarboxylase. Thus, an enzyme malfunction might also underlie Huntington's chorea. Glutamic acid, moreover, is synthesized by body cells along two pathways, one of which requires the participation of *pyridoxine*, vitamin B_6. Therefore, there is also a possibility that chorea reflects a vitamin deficiency. On the other hand, attempts to treat chorea with glutamic acid have failed. GABA itself cannot be used because it does not readily enter the brain from the *blood*.

As for epilepsy, electric shock and some drugs can provoke an attack in almost everyone whether or not they have suffered from the disease. Thus, as in the case of Huntington's chorea, other causative events must underlie epilepsy. The movement disorder called Parkinson's disease presents analogous problems. The disorder is related to a deficiency of the excitatory transmitter, *dopamine*, in the basal ganglia. A dopamine-related drug, *L-dopa*, controls parkinsonism in many patients but does not cure the disease. Because dopamine is excitatory in the basal ganglia whereas GABA is inhibitory, parkinsonism and Huntington's chorea may be looked upon as disorders associated with opposite biochemical lesions though the causes are unknown in both instances.

As an inhibitory transmitter in the limbic system, GABA reduces alertness. It may, therefore, prevent abnormal anxiety. The *tranquillizers* appear to increase the availability of GABA in relation to excitatory transmitters in the limbic system such as dopamine and *noradrenaline*.

Gastric juice (see *Hydrochloric acid, Pepsin*)

Gastrin (see *Hydrochloric acid, Pepsin*)

Globulin

A large class of *proteins* found in the *blood* which transport other substances, mediate immunity and participate in blood clotting. Except for the albumins, the globulins are the most abundant blood plasma proteins.

There are four major groups of globulins: alpha 1, alpha 2, beta and gamma. Gamma globulin is also known as immunoglobulin. The two alpha groups differ in their chemical characteristics, but both bind and carry various *lipids* and *steroids* as well as *haemoglobin* which is being transported for purposes other than gas transfer, for example, to the spleen to be broken down and recycled. The beta globulins also transport lipid, and they may carry two *minerals, copper* and *iron*. Prothrombin, one of the *blood factors* required for clotting, is a globulin.

The immunoglobulins consist of *antibodies* whereas the other globulins serve non-immune defence functions. The non-immune globulins are synthesized in the liver, but the immunoglobulins are synthesized by lymphocytes, cells which make up the *lymph* system. Because they are antibodies, these globulins may be used clinically to transfer immunity temporarily from a person who has recovered from an infectious disease such as measles to protect a person who wishes to avoid the illness. This immunity is passive because the measles antibodies are received by the subject. It is temporary because the subject is not challenged by the measles *antigen* to produce his own antibodies. On the other hand, vaccination confers an active, long-term immunity.

However, only two of the four or five sub-groups of immunoglobulins confer temporary passive immunity. They are identified as IgM and IgG. IgA is thought to be excreted through mucous membranes to counter invading viruses or toxins. IgE sensitizes the large population of mast cells in all parts of the body and similar basophil cells in the blood. These cells secrete *heparin* and the amines, *histamine* and *serotonin* which cause changes in the circulation of the blood. Heparin reduces the tendency of blood to clot, and the amines cause the walls of small blood vessels, especially the capillaries, to become more porous. When the same antigen enters the tissues again, mast and basophil cells pour out these substances causing the severe reactions known as allergy and anaphylaxis. Anaphylaxis is an extreme allergic response affecting about 1 in 10 of those who suffer from allergies. An anaphylactic reaction can cause fatal constriction of the air passages in the lungs. Heparin and the amines secreted by mast and basophil cells also appear to be the beginning of the inflammatory process, but the non-immune defence globulins can also bring about inflammation. Injuries too are known to stimulate mast cells and basophils to begin the secretion of a series of inflammatory products (see also *leukotriene, prostaglandin*).

An IgD group of immunoglobulins has also been identified, but its function is unclear. The classification of immunoglobulins depends on their size and weight, and on the *amino acids* forming their constant segments (see *antibody*).

Glucagon

A *hormone* secreted in the pancreas which helps to regulate the availability of *glucose* for energy (see *citric acid*).

Glucagon works principally in the liver causing the breakdown of *glycogen* to glucose. In *fat* tissue, it catalyzes the conversion of *lipids* to products essential for energy formation. In the pancreas, glucagon is synthesized by cells in the islets of Langerhans (Paul Langerhans, German pathologist, 1847–88) called A cells. The islets are distinctive bodies within pancreatic tissue consisting of three types of cells: A cells, B cells which secrete *insulin* and D cells which may regulate both glucagon and insulin by the secretion of *somatostatin*. All three hormones play a role in maintaining the correct *blood* and tissue levels of glucose given the current state of the body. Indeed, the islet cells may be regulated in part by the involuntary nervous system, thus assuring quick response to a rapidly changing situation (see also *transmitter*).

Glucagon activates *cyclic adenosine monophosphate* within liver cells, initiating a series of steps that lead to the breakdown of glycogen and a rise in the level of blood sugar. Thus, it acts roughly in opposition to insulin which lowers blood sugar by facilitating the uptake of glucose by cells and the formation of glycogen in the liver.

Diabetes mellitus, a severe disorder of the glucose-regulating mechanism, may be caused in part by overproduction of glucagon. Insulin secretion in these patients could be approximately normal, but it would be overbalanced by glucagon. Treatment would consist of a drug that inhibits glucagon secretion.

Glucose

A simple *sugar* or monosaccharide. In the body, glucose is the storage form in which all *carbohydrates* are made available to cells for conversion to energy. It occurs naturally in honey, grapes and a few other foods, but its most common dietary sources are starch and sucrose or common white table sugar. Starch consists of long chains of linked glucose molecules. Sucrose is a disaccharide in which glucose is combined with another sugar, *fructose*. Glucose is only about half as sweet to the taste as sucrose. It can be synthesized in the body from other carbohydrates and from *fat* and *protein*.

Much of the glucose absorbed from the intestine is carried by the *blood* to the liver. It is stored in the liver and in muscles after it has been converted to *glycogen* or animal starch. Glycogen, like starch, is a long chain of linked glucose molecules, but it differs from starch in the way the glucose molecules are linked together. Starch contains two forms of glucose linkage: amylose which takes up a helical conformation, and amylopectin in long, straight, branching chains. Glycogen lacks amylose. Incidentally, cellulose also consists of long glucose-linked chains and is the principal plant storage form of sugar, but unlike those of the cow for example, human digestive *enzymes* cannot break down cellulose. Pure glucose is no better as a source of energy than sucrose or starch although it may be absorbed into the blood more quickly.

Of the glucose carried in the blood for circulation, about 20 per cent and as high as 50 per cent in infants is taken up by the brain cells for conversion to energy. The rest is used by muscles and other tissues.

When glucose is required from storage, glycogen is

broken down with the catalytic intervention of the enzyme, phosphorylase (see also *adrenocorticotropic hormone*). The first step is formation of an activated molecule, glucose-1-phosphate. The number refers to the carbon atom to which the phosphate is attached (see structural formula, below). The molecule is now activated because the phosphate link is itself a source of energy. In the next step, a second enzyme, phosphoglucomutase, moves the phosphate to carbon atom 6 forming glucose-6-phosphate, which is in turn converted to glucose via the enzyme, glucose-6-phosphatase. Glucose from the blood must be reconverted in cells to glucose-6-phosphate, and this compound goes through four more steps before it enters the *citric acid* cycle for conversion to energy. In muscle cells, glucose-6-phosphate may also be broken down quickly in the absence of *oxygen* by another, less-efficient energy-making process to produce lactic acid. In yeast a similar process, fermentation, converts glucose to alcohol.

The usual structural formula for glucose found in the body is:

The numbers in circles (①) show the customary numbering of the carbon atoms.

Glutamic acid

An *amino acid* which may serve any one of three functions: (1) as a constituent of *protein* (2) as the precursor of *gamma-amino butyric acid* (GABA) and (3) as a *transmitter* of signals between nerve cells in the brain cortex.

Perhaps the most interesting question raised by this versatile molecule, one to which there is no clear answer, is how a nerve cell decides which use it will make of its limited store of glutamic acid molecules. Will they be used to synthesize new *enzymes* or structural proteins? Will they be converted to GABA, itself a transmitter although in a part of the brain outside the cortex? Or will it be used by cortical cells at least, as a transmitter?

Glutamic acid is synthesized by cells of non-nervous tissue too. The two possible synthetic pathways are the same in all cells: either ammonia is added to a *carbohydrate*, oxoglutarate, or another amino acid is added to the same carbohydrate. The latter combination is catalyzed by an enzyme which uses *pyridoxine*, vitamin B_6, as a *coenzyme*.

Glutamic acid is found within the folic acid molecule. It is also a component of the food additive, monosodium glutamate. In the body, it can be converted to *glucose* – yet another possible use for this small molecule. If the conversion does take place, the *nitrogen* in glutamic acid is used either to synthesize other amino acids, or it is converted to the waste product, *urea*.

Glycerol (see *Carbohydrate*, *Lipid*)

Glycine

The smallest *amino acid* performs several possible functions: (1) as a constituent of *protein*, (2) as a precursor of both the nucleic acids (see *deoxyribonucleic acid, ribonucleic acid*), (3) as a precursor of *porphyrin*, a class of chemicals in *cytochrome* and *haemoglobin*, (4) as a *transmitter* of signals between nerve cells in the brain cortex, and (5) as an agent capable of combining with toxic substances to render them harmless.

Glycine may also be converted into other amino acids, and it can be synthesized from them. It is a potential source of *glucose*, a transformation catalyzed by an *enzyme* which requires the *vitamin, folic acid*, as a *coenzyme*. The question of how a cell determines its use of glycine cannot yet be answered, but the balance of relevant chemicals in the cell's environment probably somehow plays a role.

In the synthesis of nucleic acids, glycine contributes atoms to the purine *bases, adenine* and *guanine*. One example of the detoxifying role played by glycine is its combination in the liver (where most detoxifications occur) with benzoic acid from the diet to form hippuric acid. The latter is then excreted in the urine.

As a transmitter of nerve signals, glycine inhibits the activity of the cell receiving it, slowing or even stopping the movement of the signal. A malfunction in synthesis or the misuse of glycine could underlie epilepsy, a disease which reflects abnormal spread of excitation from some focal point in the brain cortex (see also *gamma-amino butyric acid*).

The customary structural formula for glycine is:

$$CH_2—NH_2$$
$$|$$
$$COOH$$

Glycogen

The storage form of *glucose* in humans and many other animals. Also called animal starch to distinguish it from ordinary starch, a storage form of glucose in plants. Glycogen is a fuel reserve found principally in the liver and in muscles. The average adult body contains about two pounds of glycogen.

In the liver, glycogen is converted to glucose under the influence of the *hormone, glucagon*. Its deposition in both liver and muscle cells is enhanced by *insulin* and by corticosteroid hormones (see *hydrocortisone*) which cause cells to synthesize glucose from *protein*. In muscle, glycogen is converted to glucose principally under the influence of *adrenaline* and the thyroid hormone, *thyroxine*. As soon as it is broken down to glucose, muscular glycogen is utilized for energy.

Because it contains thousands of molecules of glucose, glycogen is a *carbohydrate* and a polysaccharide or multiple *sugar*. It is arranged in long, branching chains, thus:

Growth hormone (GH Somatrophin, STH)

A *protein* synthesized and secreted by cells of the pituitary gland below the mid-brain in the bony roof of the mouth. As the name suggests, growth hormone helps to regulate growth. Under-production of the hormone can cause dwarfism. Overproduction, which can be caused by a pituitary tumour, has different effects depending on the age of the patient. In children whose long *bones* are not yet fully developed, the arms and legs grow excessively, a condition known appropriately as giantism. In adults, overproduction of growth hormone leads to excessive enlargement of the bones of the face and pelvis, a grossly-deforming condition called acromegaly (Gr.: *akron* = extremity + *megas* = great).

Height and body size depend on inherited factors, but many genes (see *deoxyribonucleic acid* (DNA)) are probably involved in the ultimate product and the environment also plays a significant role. No doubt one of the relevant genes causes pituitary cells to synthesize growth hormone, inasmuch as proteins are the direct product of gene expression (see DNA, *ribonucleic acid*). The hormone acts to increase circulating *glucose* as do *adrenaline*, *glucagon* and the corticosteroids such as *hydrocortisone*. Growth hormone also promotes *nitrogen* retention reducing loss of that element in *urea* and urine. Thus, more nitrogen-containing *amino acids* are available for protein synthesis, an essential element in cell multiplication – that is, growth.

Growth hormone is secreted by the pituitary in response to a *releasing factor* from nerve cells in the hypothalamus, the mid-brain region to which the pituitary is attached. The releasing-factor secretion is inhibited by another chemical, *somatostatin*. This hormone may also be synthesized by hypothalamic cells, but it is certainly produced by cells of the islets of Langerhans in the pancreas. Because of the close proximity of the islet cells secreting somatostatin to those secreting glucagon and *insulin*, it seems probable that growth hormone output is regulated in part by the energy needs of the whole body at any given time.

Growth hormone is found in all mammals, but despite the similarities of the molecules, it is a species-specific chemical. Only human growth hormone affects changes in the human body, though some monkey GH may also be a useful drug in cases of hormone underproduction. The protein has been synthesized, but GH for drug use is taken primarily from pituitary extracts. The effects of underproduction in children can be corrected. Overproduction, on the other hand, is not so simply dealt with. It is usually necessary to determine and correct the cause of the overproduction. Of course, improper or slow growth may well reflect other factors than growth-hormone deficiency, notably dietary inadequacies.

Guanine

A *base* found in some *nucleotides* and in the nucleic acids, *deoxyribonucleic acid* (DNA) and *ribonucleic acid*. In the DNA double helix, the complement of guanine is *cytosine*; that is, guanine in one DNA molecule attracts and binds cytosine in the second strand of the helix. In nucleotides, guanine and *ribose*, guanosine, combine with from one to three phosphates.

Guanine is found in all food and can be synthesized by body cells. The molecule consists of a six-place ring (see Appendix 1) bound to a five-place imidazole ring, and is therefore one of the class of chemicals called purines.

Haemoglobin (Hb)

A large *protein* molecule which carries *oxygen* to the tissues and by a different mechanism helps to remove *carbon dioxide* from the tissues.

Detailed analysis of the large, complex molecule was one of the earliest important successes of the techniques that have made possible the new science of molecular biology. The work was done by M. F. Perutz, a German scientist working at Cambridge, and his associates during the early 1960s. Perutz and his student, J. C. Kendrew, won the Nobel Prize for chemistry in 1962 for this and related research.

A haemoglobin molecule consists of four relatively loosely linked protein molecules, two so-called alpha chains and two beta chains. Each alpha chain is like every other alpha chain, and in the same way, each beta chain is like every other beta chain. Each one of the four proteins, moreover, contains tightly bound within itself a haem molecule containing an *iron* atom at its centre:

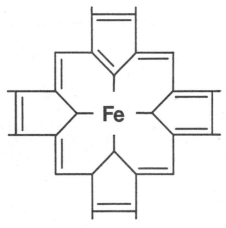

Additional atoms and atomic groups are attached to the ends of the lines shown without connections in the diagram.

Haem is a *porphyrin* consisting of *carbon, hydrogen, oxygen* and *nitrogen*, but it is the iron atom which transports oxygen. In fact, the iron exists as an *ion*, and it combines loosely with two atoms of oxygen in the presence of air in the lungs. The oxygen is released when the oxygen content of the haemoglobin in the *blood* is greater than that in the tissues through which the blood is circulating. The iron ion does not change during the transaction.

Because of the atomic forces exerted by the atoms in their constituent *amino acids*, each of the four proteins forming haemoglobin is twisted so that two histidine amino acids are juxtaposed. The haem molecule in each chain is held between the two histidines in such a way that a gap is left large enough to admit oxygen molecules; that is, O_2. When haemoglobin takes up oxygen in the lungs, the whole molecule shrinks very slightly, shortening interatomic distances. Then, when the oxygen is released in the tissues, the whole molecule expands again. In its expanded state, the exposed ends of the four protein chains form temporary compounds with the carbon dioxide which has diffused into the blood through the thin capillary walls. The greater pressure of CO_2 in tissues as a result of cellular activity causes the gas to diffuse into the blood. At the same time, the loss of oxygen to the tissues allows the haemoglobin to take up the CO_2. Haemoglobin is not the only blood protein able to carry CO_2, however, and some CO_2 is transported in the plasma in combination with *hydrogen* ions (see *carbonic acid*).

The relationship between the amounts of the two gases carried by the blood is complex. On the whole, the more O_2 in the blood, the more CO_2 it can carry. Under normal conditions of resting breathing, the blood stays in contact with air in the lungs for only about three-quarters of a second. In the tissues, roughly a fifth of the blood-borne oxygen is released. As CO_2 pressure builds up in the tissues, moreover, it is sensed by special nerve cells which inform brain centres regulating breathing. Thus, CO_2 pressure regulates lung activity rather than oxygen need as such, but in any case, the gas balance is related to the body's fluctuating requirements. Because the blood moves, furthermore, gas exchange in the lungs and other tissues always occurs between tissues in motion relative to each other. Finally, the amount of oxygen and carbon dioxide in the blood is regulated by the *acid-base* balance which the two gases do much to establish. Oxygenated haemoglobin allows the blood to accept more carbon dioxide because it is a buffer against acidity. At the same time, oxygenated haemoglobin being less capable of carrying CO_2, more of the gas may enter the plasma, increasing its relative acidity. When the body is at rest, blood carries roughly a litre of oxygen, but determination of blood gas content is extremely hard and usually inexact.

The colour of the blood derives directly from the iron ions at the centre of the haem molecules. When it is carrying oxygen, haemoglobin gives blood its familiar bright red, arterial colour. The bluish-red, venous colour appears when oxygen content is reduced. Poor circulation causes blood movement to slow so that oxygen content falls. Strangulation produces the same effect, and the skin becomes blue, a condition called cyanosis (Gr.: *kyanos* = blue).

If the blood contains carbon monoxide, the colour becomes cherry red and a bright red flush appears in the skin. Carbon monoxide kills by strangulation. It combines with the haem iron to form a far more stable compound than the normal combination of haem with oxygen. What is more, the affinity of haem for carbon monoxide is 250 times greater than its affinity for oxygen. As little as 0.1 per cent carbon monoxide in the air can be fatal. Up to 5 per cent of the haem in the blood of heavy smokers, they should note, may be permanently bound to carbon monoxide.

Normal human haemoglobin exists in two forms: adult haemoglobin (HbA) and foetal haemoglobin (HbF). The alpha chains in both are the same, but there are slight differences in the amino-acid sequences of the respective beta chains. In HbF, the beta chains – here called gamma chains! – are better able to take up oxygen at lower pressure, a necessary adaptation because foetal blood is oxygenated by the mother's lungs and must pass through the placenta. The change from HbF to HbA begins at birth and should be completed by the age of four.

Errors in the structure of haemoglobin chains may cause serious anaemias or other disorders. Most such errors are inherited. They occur because of a mistake in the structure of a gene which causes an error in the amino-acid sequence of the protein (see *deoxyribonucleic acid*).

One of the most common causes the disease known as sickle-cell anaemia. Sickle-cell haemoglobin (HbS) differs from normal HbA in only one amino acid in each of the two beta chains, the substitution of a valine for one *glutamic acid*. The effect is to give the molecule a shorter life. Red blood cells containing HbS are sickled rather than round in shape, moreover, and tend to be abnormally 'brittle' and easily damaged. The disease occurs in many tropical regions where it affects almost 40 per cent of the population, a state of affairs that seems at first glance to contradict Darwinism. The responsible gene is dominant; that is, it will almost certainly make its effect felt in the offspring even when only one parent carries it. If it is inherited from both parents, the chance of early death is high, but if the HbS gene comes from only one parent, only part of the haemoglobin is malformed and the child may live to marry and have children. Yet under most circumstances, a gene that puts its bearer at a disadvantage with respect to the whole population will die out because the disadvantaged individuals die earlier. In the regions where sickle-cell anaemia flourishes, however, malaria is endemic. The malaria parasite must live part of its life cycle in the patient's red blood cells, but for some reason, it cannot survive in sickled cells. Thus, sickled-cell victims are protected against malaria, a much more widespread killer. Unexpectedly, the sickle-cell gene provides a definite advantage in malarial regions.

Thalassaemia or Cooley's anaemia is also a disease caused by a genetic error. It is found principally in the eastern Mediterranean (Gr.: *thalassa* = sea). This form of the disorder also affects the beta proteins, but there are alpha-thalassaemias in which the alpha protein is malformed. Like sickle-cell anaemia, now sometimes called beta-thalassaemia, it is always fatal at an early age when the malformed gene has been inherited from both parents, but the victim may survive to have children if the disorder is inherited from only one parent. Its effect is to cause HbF to persist into adult life. The HbF red blood cells are more fragile than HbA cells, and not enough new HbF is synthesized to make up for the greater loss. Why thalassaemia exists despite this severe disadvantage is unknown.

Yet another group of very rare haemoglobin diseases is known collectively as porphyria. Again, they are genetic disorders, but they are caused by the malfunction of enzymes involved in biosynthesis of porphyrin (see above). In all forms of porphyria, an excess of porphyrins are excreted often causing urine and faeces to take on vivid shades of purple or red. Symptoms also include anaemia, abdominal disorders and mental disturbances. The anaemia seems to be caused by the loss of malformed haem and the relative absence of normal molecules. Porphyria is not usually immediately fatal, but it cannot be cured. Treatment is confined to easing the symptoms.

Normal haem destruction takes place in the spleen and liver. The iron is retained, and the porphyrins become part of the *bile*, or they are broken down and excreted in urine.

For other kinds of anaemia, see *folic acid, cyanocobalamin*.

Hapten (see *Antigen*)

Heparin

A *hormone* which inhibits blood clotting (see *blood factor*), and with the *enzyme, lipase*, helps to clear *fat* particles from the *blood*. Because it acts in the immediate vicinity of cells that synthesize it, heparin is known as a local hormone. It is found in the liver – whence its name (Gr.: *hepar* = liver) – lungs, spleen, kidneys and the small intestine. In connective tissue, it is secreted by mast cells which also synthesize *histamine*.

Purified from animal tissues, heparin is used as a drug to reduce the risk of heart attacks by preventing thrombosis; that is, blockage of a blood vessel by a clot. Heparin must be injected because like other large polysaccharide molecules (see *carbohodrate, sugar*), it is broken down by *saliva* and stomach acids. Newer anticoagulant drugs consist of entirely different substances which can be taken orally.

Heparin is a mucopolysaccharide, a long chain of sugar molecules each of which contains an amino group (see *amino acid*). It was identified in the 1920s but has never been described in detail. It acts to prevent the formation of thrombin and fibrin, but the mechanism of action at the molecular level is unknown.

Histamine

A *hormone* the effects of which differ with the tissue in which it acts. In the skin and lungs, histamine causes an allergy-like inflammatory reaction. In the stomach, it causes an increase in the secretion of *hydrochloric acid* and *pepsin*. It is synthesized in connective tissue throughout the body by mast cells which also secrete *heparin*. Because histamine acts in the immediate vicinity of cells that secrete it, it is called a local hormone.

In skin and muscle, mast cells secrete histamine in response to injury or the appearance of *globulins*. The hormone causes the walls of capillaries and other small blood vessels to become slightly porous. The effect is to allow greater seepage of plasma into the tissues to lower blood pressure. Swelling and pain follow. Histamine is also a direct pain stimulant because it excites sensory nerve endings. By the same process, it causes itching. Pain and swelling are often accompanied by heat and redness from the increased blood flow through the area. Redness, swelling, pain and heat are the four classical signs of inflammation. It now appears that histamine is the first substance to be produced by an irritant or *antigen* in a sequence of chemical events leading to inflammation not all of the steps in which are yet clear (see also *leukotriene, prostaglandin*). An analogous reaction to histamine occurs in the lungs where it initiates the constriction of the small air passages. The result is an asthmatic attack.

Anti-histamine drugs are used to combat these allergy-like inflammatory reactions which are due to the stimulation of one type of histamine *receptor* (H_1) on target cells. They do not inhibit increased synthesis of hydrochloric acid and pepsin stimulated by histamine because another type of receptor (H_2) for the hormone occurs in stomach-wall cells. Anti-histamines may act by competing with the hormone for H_1 receptors which would otherwise take up histamine, thereby blocking them against the hormone. Drugs that block H_2 receptors do not affect the allergy-like responses to histamine of *skin* and lung cells.

Histamine is an *amino acid* with the structural formula:

$$NH_2 \text{---} CH_2CH_2 \text{---}$$

It is synthesized from another amino acid, histidine.

Hormone (*Gr.: hormon = impelling*)

(Gr.: *hormon* = impelling)

(1) A chemical secreted into the *blood* which acts on cells elsewhere in the body. (2) A chemical secreted by a cell or group of cells which diffuses in the *body fluids* to act on other cells whether nearby or distant. The first is the classical definition of hormone, but the second is now more common usage. Note that digestive *enzymes* may also work at some distance from cells that secrete them, but hormones effect changes in cell functions whereas enzymes alter the structures of molecules.

There may be terminological confusion, however, at the interface between nerve-cells or neurons and hormone-secreting cells. Definition (1) includes *releasing factors* produced by the hypothalamus, a part of the mid-brain, to stimulate secretion of pituitary hormones. Definition (2) includes *transmitters*, the chemicals which carry nervous signals from one neuron to the next. At the point where a neuron touches a muscle cell, moreover, the transmitter carries a signal from a neuron effecting a change in another type of cell. Finally, definition (2) includes local hormones, those that act on cells near the cells which secrete them. At least three local hormones, *gamma-amino butyric acid*, *noradrenaline* and *serotonin*, are also transmitters. Releasing factors act like transmitters because they carry a signal from a neuron in the hypothalamus to a cell in the pituitary which releases a hormone. In the present state of knowledge, this confusion cannot be helped.

Like the nervous system, hormones co-ordinate the functions of diverse organs and tissues throughout the body. Many hormones are under the direct control of the brain. Others are not. Insulin, for example, is secreted in response to a rise in the amount of *glucose* in the blood. Neurons in the brain respond to sensory inputs with signals that prick up the ears and contract blood vessels to raise blood pressure. The same sensory inputs cause a releasing factor from the hypothalamus to stimulate secretion of *adrenocorticotropic hormone* (ACTH) by the anterior or forward pituitary. ACTH in turn directs the secretion of corticosteroids from the cortex of the adrenal glands. The sensory input may also stimulate *adrenaline* production from the adrenal medulla through the intermediation of the sympathetic nervous system (see *transmitter*). Adrenaline intensifies the condition of alertness preparatory to attack or self-defence. Hormones might be looked upon as a second order of body co-ordinating signals, slower than neurons but with more lasting effects.

The classical hormones (definition (1)) are all produced by endocrine glands; that is, ductless glands with cells that secrete directly into the blood. Exocrine glands are those with ducts leading, for example, into the intestine. Thus, the pancreas consists of both endocrine glandular tissues, the islets of Langerhans (Paul Langerhans, German pathologist, 1847–88), and exocrine tissue which secretes digestive enzymes such as *chymotrypsin*. The endocrine glands are:

(1) The pituitary, about the size of a pea, located in the bony roof of the mouth. It is attached by a stalk of neurons to the hypothalamus and is a part of the brain. In man, the pituitary has two segments, the posterior pituitary or neurohypophysis and the anterior pituitary or adenohypophysis.

(2) Adrenals, two small caps, each sitting on top of a kidney. The adrenal gland has a cortex and a medulla or centre. Each part secretes its own hormones.

(3) The islets of Langerhans in the pancreas. In slides of pancreatic tissue examined under a microscope, the islets are clearly separated from and surrounded by the rest of the pancreatic tissue.

(4) Thyroid, a large gland just inside the hollow above the breast *bone*.

(5) The parathyroid, as the name implies, just behind the thyroid. It consists of four small, separate glands.

(6) The gonads; that is, testes or ovaries.

(7) Thymus which secretes thymosin. It plays an important if poorly understood role in the immune defence system, especially in 'teaching' immune defence cells, the lymphocytes, to recognize *antigens* in the same body so that the cells will not form *antibodies* capable of attacking body antigens.

(8) The pineal, also a cluster of neurons at almost the exact centre of the brain. Its function in humans is uncertain and controversial.

The table lists hormones alphabetically, the tissues where each is secreted, target tissues and physiological function. Local hormones are identified as (LO). Excepting for

> Calcitonin (see *calcium*)
> Cholecystokinin (see *bile*)
> Gastrin (see *hydrocholoric acid*)
> Kallidin (see *bradykinin*)
> Thymosin (see above)

all of these substances are described in their own entries.

Hormone (Abbreviation, other names)	Origin	Target organ	Function
Adrenaline	Adrenal medulla	All tissues, esp. heart, blood vessels	'Fight-or-flight' preparation
Adrenocortico-tropic hormone (ACTH)	Pituitary, ant.	Adrenal cortex	Stim. secretion of corticosteroids
Aldosterone	Adrenal cortex	Kidneys	Acid–base balance
Angiotensin (LO)	Blood	Smooth muscle, esp. blood vessels	Incr. blood pressure
Bradykinin (LO)	Blood	Smooth muscle, esp. blood vessels	Decr. blood pressure
Calcitonin	Thyroid	Bone, teeth, nails	Incr. blood calcium level

Hormone (Abbreviation, other names)	Origin	Target organ	Function
Cholecystokinin	Small intestine	Gall bladder	Bile release
Erythropoietin (LO)	Bone marrow	Bone marrow	Red blood cell formation
Follicle-stimulating hormone (FSH)	Pituitary, ant.	Gonads	Prepare ovum, sperm development
Gamma-amino butyric acid (GABA) (LO)	Neurons	Neurons	Inhibits signals
Gastrin	Stomach: pyloric antrum	Stomach wall	Stimulates hydrochloric acid secretion
Glucagon	Pancreas: islets	Liver	Glycogen breakdown
Growth hormone (GH, Somatrophin, STH)	Pituitary, ant.	Probably all tissue	Normal growth
Heparin (LO)	Liver, kidneys, lungs, spleen, small intestine	Blood factors	Inhibits blood clotting
Histamine (LO)	Mast cells, most tissues	All tissues	Inflammatory, allergic reactions
Hydrocortisone	Adrenal cortex	Prob. all tissues	Glucose utilization, tissue integrity
Insulin	Pancreas: islets	Prob. all tissues	Glucose utilization
Interstitial-cell-stimulating hormone (ICSH)	Pituitary, ant.	Testes	Fertility
Kallidin (LO)	As Bradykinin		
Leukotriene (LO)	All tissues	All tissues	Inflammatory, contraction of smooth muscle
Luteinizing hormone (LH)	Pituitary, ant.	Ovary	Fertility

Hormone (Abbreviation, other names)	Origin	Target organ	Function
Melanocyte-stimulating hormone (MSH)	Pituitary	Skin, hair, nipples	Pigmentation
Melatonin	Pineal	Skin (frogs), ovaries (rats, birds)	Humans: unknown
Noradrenaline (LO)	Neurons	Neurons	Excite signals
Oestrogen	Ovary	Prob. all tissues	Female characteristics
Oxytocin	Pituitary, post.	Uterus, gut, breasts	Stimulates smooth muscle
Parathormone	Parathyroid	Blood, bone, teeth, nails	Blood calcium level, calcium stores
Progesterone	Ovary, placenta	Probably all tissues	Female characteristics, prepare uterus for ovum
Prolactin	Pituitary, ant.	Breasts	Breast development, lactation
Prostaglandin (LO)	All tissues	All tissues	Inflammation, pain, smooth muscle contraction
Releasing factors (RF)	Hypothalamus	Pituitary, ant.	Secretion of pituitary hormones
Renin (LO)	Kidneys	Blood	Angiotensin formation
Serotonin (LO)	Blood platelets, neurons	Blood factors, neurons	Clotting, excite nervous signals
Somatostatin	Pancreas: islets	Hypothalamus?	GH-RF inhibition
Testosterone	Testes	All tissues	Male characteristics, fertility

Hormone (Abbreviation, other names)	Origin	Target organ	Function
Thymosin	Thymus	Thymus, possibly bone marrow, spleen	Immune defence
Thyroid-stimulating hormone (TSH)	Pituitary, ant.	Thyroid	Stim. thyroid hormone secretion
Thyroxine	Thyroid	Probably all tissues	Normal growth, response to temperature change, lactation
Vasopressin (Antidiuretic hormone, ADH)	Pituitary, post.	Hypothalamus, kidneys, blood vessels	Temperature regulation, urine retention, incr. blood pressure

Hyaluronic acid

A large *carbohydrate* molecule found in skin, joints, connective tissue, the *vitreous humour* in the eye and in the umbilical cord. Hyaluronic acid is usually bound to *protein*. It is thought to form a gelatinous matrix uniting cells, as in the walls of *blood* capillaries. Thus, it tends to slow the spread of infectious agents and inflammatory substances such as *histamine*.

In addition, hyaluronic acid forms part of the coating surrounding and protecting ova. It adds much of the viscosity to body fluids, notably the *synovial fluid* in the joints and the vitreous humour. Synovial fluid contains only about .02 per cent to .05 per cent but acquires 80 per cent of its viscosity from this minute amount of hyaluronic acid.

When the chemical is missing or malformed, bleeding and arthritis may follow. Hyaluronic acid is normally broken down by the *enzyme*, hyaluronidase. Arthritic swelling of the joints often reflects overactivity of the enzyme, but the cause of this malfunction is not known. Hyaluronidase in seminal fluid (see *semen*) assists the sperm to enter the ovum.

Hyaluronic acid consists of a long chain of six-*carbon sugar* molecules. To every second sugar is added a *nitrogen* atom plus an acetyl group (CH_2, see Appendix 1).

Hydrochloric acid

A strong *acid* formed in the walls of the stomach to assist in the digestive process. It helps to break down both *carbohydrates* and *proteins*.

Hydrochloric acid is a very small molecule (HCl) which releases *hydrogen ions* freely and is extremely corrosive (see pH, Appendix 2). If it was formed within cells, the acid could easily disrupt cell membranes and the cellular machinery. The stomach wall itself is protected by a layer of *mucus*. Nevertheless, if the concentration of HCl in the stomach is abnormally high, ulcers may occur.

The control of so powerful a chemical is obviously essential. It is actually formed in tubes leading from oxyntic cells in the stomach wall to the interior of the stomach. Oxyntic cells concentrate both hydrogen ions, obtained from *carbonic acid*, and chloride ions (see *chlorine*). The chloride enters the cell as part of an energy-requiring carrier mechanism which also excretes another negative ion, carbonate. Two energy-requiring pumps force the hydrogen and chloride ions, respectively, out of the cell into the tube where they are able to combine for the first time as hydrochloric acid. The nature of the carrier mechanisms, the pumps and the compartmentalization maintained within the cell itself is unclear.

Hydrochloric acid is not synonymous with gastric acid which also consists of *pepsin*. The gastric juice contains gastric acid plus mucus and various *blood* group substances.

Secretion of hydrochloric acid and probably also of pepsin is regulated in part by gastrin, a *hormone* secreted by cells in the exit from the stomach, the pyloric antrim. Food in the stomach causes gastric acid secretion, and indeed, the sight and smell of food often induces the brain to signal stomach wall cells via the vagus nerve to secrete hydrochloric acid. The vagal connection, a part of the sympathetic nervous system (see *transmitter*), probably explains the psychic element so often apparent in the appearance of stomach ulcers.

Hydrocortisone

A *hormone* synthesized by cells in the cortex of the adrenal glands on top of the kidneys. Hydrocortisone participates in regulation of several functions including the availability of *fat* and *glucose* for energy, the release of potentially destructive *enzymes* by the cells in which they are synthesized and possibly the smooth operation of nerve cells or neurons, especially in the brain.

Hydrocortisone is a glucocorticoid; that is, it is synthesized in the adrenal cortex and is concerned with the utilization of glucose. *Aldosterone*, on the other hand, is a mineralocorticoid because although it too is secreted by the adrenal cortex, its role is regulation of the *mineral* content of *body fluids*.

Hydrocortisone is synthesized in response to stimulation of the cortical cells by *adrenocorticotropic hormone* (ACTH) released from the pituitary gland. ACTH is secreted after stimulation of the pituitary by corticotropic *releasing factor* (CRF), a chemical synthesized by cells in the hypothalamus, a mid-brain region to which the pituitary is attached. CRF in turn is produced in response to signals from brain neurons excited by a situation such as a threat. Secretion of CRF stops when the *blood* level of hydrocortisone reaches an appropriate, preset level. Thus, the hormone acts as its own feedback mechanism.

In the absence of hydrocortisone, cellular utilization of fat and glucose may become inefficient, impairing cellular energy production. Hydrocortisone seems to prepare the way for the supercharging effects of *adrenaline*. Without hydrocortisone, muscles are weakened. *Bone* formation may be subnormal. It is thought that these disorders reflect the anti-inflammatory activity of the hormone which restricts enzymes capable of loosening connective tissue and cartilage and destroying cells. Hydrocortisone stabilizes the fat-like membranes of intra-cellular sacks called lysosomes which contain minute quantities of such enzymes. Normally, the enzyme molecules are combined inside the lysosome with foreign material which is destroyed. If the lysosome is weak, however, the enzyme is released inside the cell, killing it, or inappropriately into the tissue causing damage. It was because of its anti-inflammatory role that hydrocortisone was first used as a drug to control arthritis, a disease in which the inflammatory process produces pain and swelling.

The role of hydrocortisone in neurons is controversial and even less well understood. It may alter the synthesis of *gamma-amino butyric acid* and *serotonin*, both *transmitters* of signals between neurons in the brain. Hydrocortisone could also affect the cement holding together the cells that form capillary walls, thus changing the movement of blood both in the brain and in other parts of the body, but indirectly altering brain function.

The role of hydrocortisone as a drug has been restricted by its numerous undesirable side-effects. They include an abnormal rise in blood sugar level, the unsightly redistribution of body fat, an increase in gastric acid secretion (see *hydrochloric acid, pepsin*) causing stomach ulcers, and adverse effects on the *antibody*-producing cells of the *lymph* system. Nevertheless, hydrocortisone or a synthetic chemical similar to it in structure may be used to control inflammation and in patients with chronic or acute adrenocortical insufficiency such as might be caused by a tumour of the adrenal cortex. Chemically related drugs that suppress immune defence cells are also used to prevent organ transplant rejection and to control or prevent asthma.

Like aldosterone and the sex hormones, *oestrogen, progesterone* and *testosterone*, hydrocortisone is a *steroid*. All of these hormones have very similar chemical structures. It is probable that they all act by a similar molecular mechanism and that their effects differ because they affect cells in different organs. On the other hand, it is also possible that the slight molecular differences amongst them explain their different effects. How these powerful molecules work is still uncertain.

Hydrogen

A gas, forming part of every organic compound and of water. Hydrogen is the most common *body element* in terms of numbers of atoms. As an *ion*, it determines the *acid–base* balance of *body fluids* (see pH, Appendix 2). A hydrogen ion is a single proton without the single electron usually encircling it. Therefore, it has a positive charge.

By itself, hydrogen can be a poison. It cannot produce energy either within cells or in the air except in the presence of *oxygen*.

The hydrogen ion underlies that form of bonding between atoms and molecules, the hydrogen bond, which is relatively loose and can be broken when the compound is hydrolyzed, for example, by being dissolved in water. The hydrogen bond is of the utmost importance in life. It is the basis of the double helix of *deoxyribonucleic acid*, of *protein* structure and of the bonding between some extra-cellular substances such as *enzymes*, *hormones* and *antigens* and cell *receptors*. (See also, Appendix 3.)

The lightest element, hydrogen is atomic number 1 with atomic weight 1.00797. It is colourless, odourless, tasteless and in the presence of oxygen, inflammable.

Insulin

A *hormone* secreted by cells in the islets of Langerhans (Paul Langerhans, German pathologist, 1847–88) within the pancreas. Insulin is required for normal uptake of *glucose* for conversion to energy by cells throughout the body.

Insulin causes cell membranes to become more permeable to glucose, but the molecular mechanism of this vital action is not understood. *Glucagon*, another hormone secreted by cells in the islets of Langerhans, counterbalances the action of insulin by increasing blood sugar. Two other hormones, *growth hormone* from the pituitary and *hydrocorti-*

sone from the adrenal cortex, also counterbalance insulin by promoting the breakdown of *fat* and *glycogen* stores. Insulin stimulates glycogen synthesis by liver cells. In the absence of the hormone, fat breakdown is hastened and *protein* is removed from various tissues and brought to the liver. Both fats and proteins may then be processed to form glucose as a source of energy. Thus, the storage and utilization of the principal nutrients are under complex control by several hormones. Insulin is secreted in response to the rate of change of the *blood* glucose level, and glucagon is secreted in response to the blood sugar level itself. Growth hormone secretion is regulated in part at least by the output of *somatostatin* by yet more islet cells. Glucose itself, glucagon and *serotonin* may also influence growth hormone output.

Insulin is a small protein consisting of only 51 *amino acids* (in ox insulin), with small species variations. The structure was elucidated by the British biochemist, F. Sanger, in 1960. The research earned Sanger his first Nobel Prize for chemistry. At the end of the nineteenth century, insulin had been identified as the anti-diabetic factor. In 1921 and 1922, two Canadian doctors, Banting and Best, first used a pancreatic extract from dogs to treat the disease which had until then usually been rapidly fatal.

Diabetes is now known to have two forms: early-onset and late-onset. The former appears before the age of 20 and is always associated with insulin deficiency. That is not to say that diabetes is caused by islet cell failure, however. Its causes are unknown. Insulin will control the early-onset form, but it is not a cure. Late-onset diabetes is even more baffling. It usually occurs after the age of 40 and never before 30. Insulin secretion by late-onset diabetics is often normal, or indeed, it may be excessive. Nevertheless, glucose utilization fails. Glycogen is not formed, and blood sugar levels rise characteristically. Carbohydrates called *ketones* formed by the liver from fats and proteins, moreover, disrupt the *acid–base* balance of *body fluids*. Too much of one ketone, acetoacetic acid, in the blood can impair nervous activity and lead to coma. Ketosis may also occur in early-onset diabetes, but insulin will correct the condition. In any case, ketosis may be rapidly fatal. Even in late-onset patients, a crisis brought on by ketosis may respond to insulin. For the most part, late-onset patients must control their disease by observing rigid carbohydrate-controlled diets and exercise, practices which can also be helpful to early-onset patients. Synthetic non-insulin drugs are now often used to control late-onset diabetes.

Insulin must be injected because it is a protein and is broken down in the digestive tract. Synthetic insulins are also proteins, but they remain longer in the blood.

Interferon

A group of *proteins* formed by cells in response to virus infection. Bacterial products such as some toxins may also cause cells to synthesize interferon, and artificial stimulation with a form of *ribonucleic acid* (RNA) can be used for this purpose experimentally. Interferon is one of two natural antibiotics, the other being *lysozyme*.

The interferons vary from species to species so that those synthesized by other animals cannot be used by humans. Even within the human body, different cells appear to synthesize slightly different interferons each of which works only in the cells that synthesize it. Nevertheless, interferon suitable for human cells has been successfully obtained from bacteria by the technique known as genetic engineering. In brief, the principal natural sequence – *deoxyribonucleic acid* (DNA)→RNA→protein – is reversed in the laboratory: interferon is used as a template or model to create RNA. This RNA becomes a model for DNA using an *enzyme*, reverse transcriptase. The interferon gene thus formed in DNA is then introduced into the bacterial DNA, and the bacteria synthesize human interferon. The bacteria most commonly used for this work, *Escherichia coli*, is normally found in the flora of the human gut.

It has been hoped that interferon produced by genetic engineering may be useful against some forms of cancer. Just as interferon prevents viral growth by inhibiting the formation of new viral nucleic acids (either DNA or RNA), it seems to have a similar effect on some cancer cells. The reasons why this should be the case are not clear, and so far, the success of this form of treatment is at best controversial. If suitable interferon can be obtained in sufficient quantities, however, it might also be used as a natural therapy for many kinds of viral infection, including the common cold.

Interstitial-cell-stimulating hormone (see *Luteinizing hormone*)

Intrinsic factor (see *Cyanocobalamin*)

Iodine

A trace element in the body required in *thyroxine*, a *hormone* synthesized by cells in the thyroid gland. Adequate amounts of iodine are normally obtained from food and drinking water, but in regions where there is almost no iodine in the soil, some people suffer from a large swelling at the base of the neck called goitre. Iodine-deficiency goitre (there are other kinds) is a sign of an overactive, enlarged thyroid gland struggling to make up for the hormone insufficiency by increasing the cellular productive capacity. Sea salt contains iodine and cures this kind of goitre. It is now customary to add a trace of iodine to ordinary table salt.

Iodine in alcohol solution is a strong antiseptic. It sterilizes intact skin effectively, but it is corrosive to open wounds and should not be used on cuts or open sores.

Iodine is a halogen like bromine, *chlorine* and fluorine. Its atomic number is 53, atomic weight, 126.904. It is the heaviest element found naturally in the body.

Iodopsin

One of a group of *proteins* which act as visual pigments; that is, light causes a change in the molecule which excites the cell containing it to send a signal to the brain. Light-sensitive cells are found in the retina at the back of the eyeball. Iodopsin occurs in cone cells, so called because of their shape, and a closely-related chemical, rhodopsin, occurs in rod cells.

Iodopsin is actually most sensitive to green light. There are three colour-sensitive opsins differing from each other in such a way that each responds to a different wavelength of light. Cyanopsin responds to blue, porphyrinopsin to red and iodopsin, to green. Each cone cell contains only one form of opsin, and they are the foundation of our colour vision. Its subtlety, however, is due in part to the mixing of signals from groups of cones and in part to learning.

The cone opsins are relatively less sensitive to light than rhodopsin. In other words, more light is required to cause cone cells to signal than rod cells. Though both types occur throughout the retina, cone cells are concentrated near the centre and give the point of greatest visual acuity. Rod cells occur more frequently at the outer margins of the retina and are well-adapted to detect movement at the periphery of the visual field. Their greater sensitivity to light also explains why peripheral vision is better at night than focused vision for sensing both shapes and movement.

A change in one molecule of rhodopsin brought about by the impact of the smallest unit of light, a quantum, may induce a signal in the rod cell. Light causes a shift in the location of electrons within the visual pigments so that the molecule changes its electrical properties. This shift starts the electro-chemical signal in the cell though the exact nature of the machinery that converts light to a nervous signal is not yet clear.

Once the electron shift has occurred in a visual pigment, a brief period of dark is required for the molecule to return to its receptive state. In practice, this physical fact explains the temporary blindness that can follow a flash of bright light. It also underlies the phenomenon known as dark adaptation. In darkness, the more sensitive rod cells adjust themselves to the relative absence of light and become responsive to even the dimmest light.

The visual pigments consist of a protein, opsin, plus a *coenzyme*, retinal, which is synthesized from *vitamin* A.

Ion

A charged atom. In an electrically neutral atom, the number of protons in the nucleus is balanced by the number of electrons around it. A proton has a positive charge and an electron, a negative charge. If one or more of the electrons is missing, the ion is positively charged; for example, ferrous iron, Fe^{++}, ferric iron, Fe^{+++}, sodium, Na^+. If one or more extra electrons occur, the ion is negatively charged; for example, chloride, Cl^-. Many atoms are ionized in solution in water. See also *acid, base, electrolyte*.

Iron (Fe) (L.: *ferrum*).

A metallic element required to form *haemoglobin* and the energy-transfer *protein, cytochrome*. An adult normally contains three to four grams of iron, enough to make a two-inch nail. About two thirds of the total is held in haemoglobin. Most of the balance is stored throughout the body. Small amounts occur in the cytochromes and in the *blood* plasma where the iron is bound to a protein, ferritin, for transport.

Body stores of iron are maintained almost without loss because the iron in haemoglobin is recovered and re-used when the molecule is broken down. In normal adult men, only about a milligram a day is lost, largely in sloughed skin cells. A standard western daily diet contains about 10 mg of iron. It is found especially in meat, eggs and cereals. The iron in bread is more easily absorbed if there is also vitamin C present. In other words, a glass of orange juice will assure better iron intake from the breakfast piece of toast. Absorption from food tends to match need, however. The normal absorption is about a milligram a day, but in women and children or after a haemorrhage, the body may absorb as much as 30 per cent of the dietary iron. The mechanism behind this topping-up operation is not understood.

Women lose about 30 mg of iron in the menstrual flow and, therefore, normally need roughly twice the daily adult male intake. In pregnancy of course, the mother supplies all iron required by the foetus: about 150 mg in the blood and another 250 mg in store. Pregnant women must usually receive iron supplements because the diet cannot supply enough. During breast feeding, the mother loses about a milligram a day in her *milk*. Infants and children also need about twice the normal adult male iron intake to allow for the new red blood cells needed to make up added blood volume and for increased storage.

Blood loss caused by injuries, during surgery or haemorrhage must be made good at first by transfusion of some kind, but then the patient's iron requirements also rise. Each half-teaspoonful of blood lost contains about a milligram of iron and doubles the normal daily requirement.

However they are caused, iron deficiencies mean that new red blood cells are less readily formed, and the individual becomes anaemic. Although the effect of iron anaemia on the oxygen-carrying capacity of the blood is the same as in any other anaemia (see *cyanocobalamin, folic acid*), the treatment is quite different. It is necessary to get iron into the patient. In a few people, deficiency is caused by a malfunction of the absorption mechanism. In an emergency, this form of anaemia is overcome by iron injections.

It is possible to take too much iron into the body. In adults, iron poisoning can be overcome with a drug, desferroxamine, which forms a soluble compound with iron so that the metal can be excreted in the urine. Diet control will prevent a recurrence of the poisoning. In small children, however, an iron overdose is very dangerous. A bottle of 50 iron pills can kill a child. Like all other drugs, iron tablets must be kept safely out of the reach of children.

Iron is a metal with atomic number 26 and atomic weight 55.847.

Kallidin (see *Bradykinin*)

Keratin

An insoluble *protein*, the principal constituent of hair, nails, the hard surface of the skin and the organic matrix of tooth *enamel*.

Keratin contains variable amounts of *sulphur*-bearing *amino acids*, cysteine and methionine, and a large proportion of the basic (see *base*) amino acids, tyrosine and leucine. Because of its unique molecular behaviour, it is an unusually flexible protein. When it is stretched, the secondary helical structure changes from an alpha helix with intrachain *hydrogen* bonds to a beta helix with bonds linking the helixes. When it is released, keratin returns to the original alpha-helical structure. The loss of this ability to unfold and refold is one reason why ageing skin wrinkles (see also *collagen*). Keratin is then no longer being synthesized, but the reason is not known.

Ketone

Any compound containing a carboxyl (CO) group, but usually a *carbohydrate*. Three ketones are normally found in the liver, muscles and kidneys: acetoacetic acid, acetone and beta-hydroxybutyric acid. All are carbohydrates. They are also called ketone bodies. They are intermediate products in the breakdown of stored *fat*. Fed into the *citric acid* cycle, they contribute to energy formation.

In starvation and a disease such as diabetes, however, ketones take on an altogether sinister role. Acetoacetic acid in particular causes *body fluids* to become too *acid*, leading to disturbances in kidney function and breathing. (See also *carbon dioxide*, *carbonic acid*.) These conditions alone might not be serious, but they are often found with ketotic coma, a state caused by some direct effect of acetoacetic acid on nerve cells in the brain. The coma is rapidly fatal. When a patient suffers from ketoacidosis, the breath smells of acetone. Because starvation can cause this disorder, it has been suggested that the 'odour of sanctity' is the smell of acetone in ketosis brought on by fasting.

Ketosis reflects a state of *glucose* starvation. Cells are unable to obtain or absorb glucose, and their energy production fails. Fat and eventually *protein* are broken down in the liver for conversion to glucose in order to make up a deficit that is real enough in starvation, but in diabetes reflects the disease state (see *insulin*). One intermediate product of both fat and protein breakdown, oxaloacetate, plays a crucial role. Normally, this carbohydrate combines with the acetyl group (CH_2) of acetyl coenzyme A at the start of the citric acid cycle. If it is diverted to form glucose, acetyl groups from fat breakdown combine together forming aceto-acetyl coenzyme A. A further transformation produces acetoacetic acid, and this ketone may be converted to acetone or beta-hydroxybutyric acid. In these circumstances, the ketone bodies are of no further use for energy formation and simply build up in the *blood*, eventually being excreted in the urine.

Lactose

A *sugar* consisting of *galactose* and *glucose* obtained from *milk*. Human milk contains about 14 grams of lactose in half a pint compared with about 10 grams in an equal amount of cow's milk.

In the small intestine, an *enzyme*, lactase, splits lactose into its constituent sugars which are absorbed. The galactose is converted to glucose in the liver. Lactase is synthesized in cells lining the intestinal walls, but only in Caucasians does the secretion of lactase continue after weaning. Other racial groups lose the ability to break down lactose for digestion. If non-Caucasian adults drink a large amount of milk, it ferments in the intestine through the action of intestinal bacteria and causes diarrhoea. Lactase secretion may also stop in some infantile diseases. Such children must be fed with lactose-free milk.

The presence of lactose in the gut appears to increase *calcium* absorption from food. The reason is not known.

Some fermentations convert lactose to lactic acid which clots milk *protein*, for example, thickening yoghurt. Any salt of lactic acid is lactate, a *carbohydrate* produced by the breakdown of glucose in the absence of *oxygen* to obtain energy. This pathway is used to supplement the *citric acid* cycle in muscles during exercise, but it is an inefficient source of energy.

Leukotriene

A local *hormone* closely related chemically to *prostaglandin* with powerful effects on involuntary muscles, especially in the lungs, and in the process of inflammation.

Four leukotrienes, A, B, C and D, have been identified. Only C and D are known to be active. They appear to be the first step in the constriction of muscle cells in the bronchioles, the small air passages of the lungs. Thus, they initiate an asthmatic attack. Until the leukotrienes had been identified, this initiator substance had been known only as slow-reacting substance of anaphylaxis because it causes a slow constriction leading to an acute asthmatic attack called anaphylaxis. Unlike the prostaglandins, the leukotrienes have not yet been positively identified in other inflammatory reactions in man.

The four leukotrienes differ from each other only very slightly and are all epoxides or *sulphur*-containing ethers. Leukotriene A is the precursor of the other three. All four are derived from arachidonic acid, a fatty acid (see *lipid*) which also gives rise to the prostaglandins. In the inflammatory process, the leukotrienes seem to act before the prostaglandins.

Lipase (Steapsin)

A group of *enzymes* which play an important role in *fat* and *lipid* formation or breakdown. Lipase secreted into the upper small intestine, the duodenum, by the pancreas is needed for digestion of food fats. It helps the breakdown of triglycerides, the common fat molecules, to their constituent fatty acids. In cells of adipose or fat tissue, lipase performs the same function when fatty acids are required, for example, as a source of energy. In *blood*, one of the lipases helps to

Lipid

clear fat particles through capillary walls into the tissues, but in this role the enzyme requires *heparin* as a *coenzyme*.

Lipid

A *fat*; more exactly, an organic substance insoluble in water but soluble in alcohol, ether, chloroform or other fat solvents. The word, lipid, is customarily used with reference to the biochemistry of fats whereas fat is used in connection with food content and the tissues. The two words are more or less interchangeable.

The lipids serve three main functions: (1) energy storage, (2) formation and maintenance of cell membranes and (3) as precursors of *hormones* such as the *steroid* hormones. Energy reserves are stored principally as triglycerides. A triglyceride consists of an alcohol, glycerol, combined with three molecules of fatty *acid*. Glycerol can also combine with one fatty acid forming a monoglyceride, or with two, a diglyceride, but these substances usually occur only as intermediate stages in the build up or breakdown of tri-glycerides.

The fatty acids are substances with the general formula: $CH_3(CH_2)_nCOOH$, where n is always an even number. The most common are oleic ($(CH_2)_{14}(CH)_2$), palmitic $(CH_2)_{14}$ and stearic $(CH_2)_{16}$. Oleic acid is unsaturated; that is, it contains a double bond – one only in this case, between the two CH groups, because the two *carbon* atoms are each linked to only one *hydrogen*, leaving a missing electron to be shared between them. Although fatty acids can be converted from one form to another by body cells, unsaturated fatty acids cannot be synthesized *de novo* by human cells, or by cells of many other mammals. Only linoleic acid $(CH_2)_{10}$, an unsaturated fatty acid, is 'essential' in the sense that small amounts must be obtained from the diet. The best sources are vegetable oils. In addition to its role in the formation of triglycerides, moreover, linoleic acid is a precursor of the local hormone family, the leukotrienes and *prostaglandins*.

Palmitic and stearic acid are saturated; that is, all

119

bonds are single. There is statistical evidence that the saturated fatty acids, found mostly in meat, are associated with heart and circulatory diseases whereas unsaturated fatty acids from vegetable oils are not. No explanation for such a connection has yet been advanced.

The fatty acids are hydrophobic; that is, they tend to repel water molecules electrostatically. This quality prevents fat from dissolving in water. The glycerol end of the triglyceride molecule, on the other hand, is hydrophilic. Thus, lipid molecules are amphipathic (see *bile*). Although the whole triglyceride is electrically neutral, its hydrophobic-hydrophilic duality has important consequences. It causes lipid molecules in water to line up side by side so that their hydrophilic ends face towards the water and their hydrophobic ends, away from the water. This behaviour underlies the second major function of lipids, the formation and maintenance of cell membranes.

Both *body fluids* and the interior of cells – the so-called cytoplasm – consist principally of water. Lipid molecules in cells, therefore, tend to form one of two structures: micelles or bilayers. Micelles are circles, or spheres, thus:

— hydrophobic fatty acid
O hydrophilic glycerol

The bilayer structure looks roughly like this:

In cells, potentially destructive enzymes are contained within bilayer sacks called lysosomes (see also *hydrochloric acid, interferon*), and the *transmitters* of signals between nerve cells are stored in vesicles of a similar construction.

Both the bilayer and the micellar structures can be formed with relative ease by placing a drop of olive oil on the surface of water in a glass. A light microscope is needed to inspect the result. The oil spreads out to form a single molecular layer on the still surface of the water. With a little practice, it is possible by gently agitating the surface to get the oil to form a bilayer. Micelles will appear if the oil is stirred into the water.

The bilayer is the basic structure of all cell membranes, both those surrounding the cell and those forming important intracellular organelles such as the energy transducer, the mitochondrion. The bilayers have inclusions such as lipid micelles, enzymes and other *protein* molecules. Proteins within the bilayer linked to *carbohydrates* that extend beyond it are often the cell *receptors* for hormones, transmitters and drugs. They may also act as the cell's *antigens*. Lipids combined with phosphate groups from which they obtain energy (see *adenosine triphosphate, phosphorus*) are thought to transport large molecules into and out of the cell. In nerve and muscle cells, such phospholipids, possibly in synchrony with *adenyl cyclase*, regulate the movement of *ions* which produce excitation.

The capacity of lipids to form micelles is also important in the digestion of fats. *Bile* consists of lipids which surround fat particles in the intestine so that they can be absorbed through the intestinal cell walls and into the *lymph* on the body side of the cells. The bile acts as an emulsifier analogous to soap (also principally lipid), but whereas soap emulsifies the fat in a pan and allows it to be carried away by water, the bile micelles probably combine with intestinal cell membranes. The fat particle would be released into the cell.

In their third functional role, lipids act as the precursors of steroids, including *cholesterol* and several hormones. Steroids are lipids in the sense that they are soluble in fat solvents but not in water though their structures are quite different from triglycerides.

The lipids are energy stores because they can be converted in the liver to carbohydrates. In the event of dietary deficiency or disease, they may also be used to synthesize protein, but *nitrogen*-containing compounds must also be available. The *blood* always carries some lipids in the form of triglycerides, cholesterol, phospholipids and fatty acids.

Because they are not soluble in water, these substances are transported by becoming attached to proteins which are then called lipoproteins. There are four main classes of lipoproteins distinguished by gross physical properties of the molecules such as their mobility in an electrical field and their molecular weight. The lipoproteins may malfunction, perhaps because they are improperly formed. Such disorders affect the use of fats in various organs, and they are often associated with other diseases such as diabetes and gout. In the United Kingdom, the most common lipoprotein disorder is hyperlipidproteinaemia Type IV, an excess of Type IV. The patients tend to be middle-aged men with cardiovascular disease. Their blood cholesterol is abnormally high, a condition which may be associated with accidental clotting (thrombosis) and other damage to the circulation. Dietary fats must be rigidly restricted, and carbohydrates, especially *sugar*, and alcohol are also controlled. The causes of this and related disorders are not known.

Local hormone (see *Hormone*)

Luteinizing hormone (LH; Interstitial cell-stimulating hormone, ICSH)

A *protein* to which a *sugar* is attached – that is, a glycoprotein – secreted by the pituitary gland. In women, the hormone triggers the release of an ovum from the ovarian follicle and subsequently stimulates the follicular cells remaining in the ovary. They are converted to a yellow cell mass, the corpus luteum, which secretes the hormone, *progesterone*. In men, the same chemical is called ICSH because it stimulates interstitial cells in the testes to secrete the hormone, *testosterone*.

LH (ICSH) is one of six or seven hormones produced by the forward or anterior pituitary. The gland itself is located in the bony roof of the mouth just below the hypothalamus, the mid-brain region to which it is attached. It secretes LH

(ICSH) in response to a *releasing factor* from the hypothalamus. LH releasing factor is secreted in response to a rising *blood* level of *oestrogen* during the early part of the menstrual cycle. The trigger for ICSH releasing factor is less clear. LH releasing factor secretion stops in response to the rising blood level of progesterone, and in men, secretion of ICSH releasing factor is inhibited by testosterone.

Lymph (*L.: Lympha = water*)

(L.: *lympha* = water)

A part of the *body fluid* which flows through a closed system of vessels, the lymphatics. Lymph plays a role in *fat* absorption and the immune defences of the body.

In the first instance, it is the lymph rather than the *blood* which receives fat particles absorbed through the intestinal wall and carries them throughout the body. The lymphatics in the small intestine are known as lacteals because of the milky colour imparted to the lymph in them by fat particles.

The immunological role of lymph is complex. Throughout the trunk, lymphatics are regularly interrupted by lymph nodes or glands. The lymph nodes consist in part of lymphocytes, the cells which synthesize *antibodies*. Other lymph node cells act as phagocytes or macrophages; that is, cells that ingest (Gr.: *phagein* = eat) invasive substances such as bacteria and detoxify or destroy them. The activities of both lymphocytes and phagocytes are modulated by a third cell type, a lymphocyte called a T cell because it is thought to have originated in the thymus gland in the neck (see *hormone*). Before birth and during infancy, T lymphocytes in the thymus learn to distinguish self-*antigens* from foreign *antigens*. Cells capable of synthesizing antibodies against self-antigens are killed off. How this process of selection takes place is not known. In any case, adult lymph nodes contain T cells without which the other lymphocytes and the phagocytes cannot function efficiently. Yet another population of T cells and some other lymphocytes synthesize lymphokines, large molecules which stimulate *interferon* biosynthesis, cause macrophages to move out into infected or damaged tissue and activate lymphocyte cell division. The lymphokines mobilize the immune defence armies against invasion. They are among the factors that initiate the inflammatory process (see *histamine, leukotriene*). The relations amongst these groups of lymph node cells is one of the growth areas in biology, but it is already clear that these tiny glands act both as barriers against infection from outside and limit the spread of dangerous substances inside the body.

The lymph also plays a role in balancing body fluids and *electrolytes* between blood and other extracellular fluids such as the *cerebrospinal fluid*. For example, if the lymphatics are blocked, protein is less easily drained from tissue causing a rise in osmotic pressure from blood to tissue with a relative fall in blood volume and a rise in tissue fluid volume called oedema. Oedema, observed as swelling, often occurs at the site of an injury because the lymphatics are blocked either by damage or by cells such as migrating macrophages. Lymph forms a kind of halfway station between blood and the other body fluids, adding to its protective role.

The flow of lymph is regulated in three ways: by muscle cells in the walls of some of the larger lymphatics, by the action of limb muscles, for example in the legs, in a manner analogous to the effect of the same muscles on the venous flow of blood back to the heart, and by valves in some lymphatics that prevent back flow. The lacteals actually constrict rhythmically so that there is a lymph pressure similar but by no means as great as blood pressure. There is no circulation, however, because the lymphatics form a closed but not a continuous system. Lymph is formed by diffusion and osmotic pressure from the blood and other body fluids into the lymphatics, and they empty into large veins in the upper thorax near the neck.

The lymph is largely water, but it contains about the same electrolytes as blood plasma and other body fluids. The protein content of lymph is normally less than that of plasma but more than other body fluids.

Lymphokine (see *Lymph*)

Lysozyme

An *enzyme* the principal function of which is to act as a natural antibiotic against bacteria (see also *interferon*). It attacks the cell walls of some bacteria, killing them, but unfortunately, it is not effective against massive infections because the bacteria multiply too rapidly for the available enzyme. Lysozyme is found in *tears*, nasal *mucus* and *saliva*, and in many tissues.

It was identified by Alexander Fleming, the British doctor who is better known as the discoverer of penicillin. He saw the effect of lysozyme on bacteria in nasal mucus and hoped at first that it might be used therapeutically. Because it is a *protein*, however, lysozyme is an *antigen* and causes allergy-like reactions. The enzyme is synthesized by cells in the immune defence system called macrophages.

Lysozyme is a small *protein* and one of the first to be analysed and described in detail. It acts by breaking the links between repeating *carbohydrate* units which make the long chains forming the tough walls surrounding bacteria. Lysozyme is also called muraminidase because one of the carbohydrates it attacks is muramic acid.

Magnesium (Mg)

A *mineral* required as a cofactor (see *coenzyme*) by *enzymes* involved in energy storage, and as an *ion* in the functioning of nerve and muscle cells.

The body contains about 25 grams (less than an ounce) of magnesium. About half is stored in *bones*, and the rest is used in cells. Magnesium is excreted at the rate of about 100 mg per day, and the British recommended intake is about 300 mg per day (US: 450 mg per day). More is needed during pregnancy, and when the mother is breast feeding. Wholegrain bread and cereals, winkles, whelks and coffee powder are among the better sources, but the average western diet supplies adequate amounts of magnesium.

Many antacids are magnesium *salts*. For example, epsom

salts is magnesium sulphate. Magnesium acts as a laxative because it tends to draw water out of the body. In older people, large doses can cause a *potassium* loss the symptoms of which are weakness and mental disturbance. Similarly, when it does occur, magnesium deficiency causes muscular weakness, serious nervous disorders, tetany, convulsions and eventually death.

Magnesium is a white metallic element, atomic number 12, atomic weight 24.312.

Maltose

A *sugar* each molecule of which consists of two molecules of *glucose*.

Maltose is the first product in the digestion of starch by the *enzyme, amylase* (ptyalin), in *saliva*. The sweet taste of bread or potatoes that have been well chewed and held briefly in the mouth comes from the maltose that has been formed. It is then broken down in the stomach to glucose.

Maltose is formed naturally in sprouted wheat and barley.

Manganese (Mn)

A *mineral* required in trace amounts as a cofactor (see *coenzyme*) by some *enzymes*. In animals, diets deficient in manganese can cause infertility and damage to nerves and *bone*. Deficiencies in humans have not been encountered. The best dietary sources of the mineral are wholegrain cereals, nuts, green vegetables and tea.

Manganese miners who inhale the mineral dust may display Parkinsonian-like symptoms: a halting gait and mental disorder. Drugs that help to remove metals from the body offer a good chance of recovery.

Manganese is a metal, atomic number 25, atomic weight, 54.938.

Melanin

(Gr.: *melas* = black)

A dark brown pigment in hair, nipples, the aureoles of the breasts and anus and in skin cells called melanocytes. All racial types have some melanocytes in their skins, but in black- and brown-skinned people, the cells produce more melanin that they do in light-skinned people. Sunlight causes melanin to be synthesized in several steps from the *amino acid*, tyrosine, thus causing tanning in light-skinned people. Freckles and age spots are also evidence of melanocyte activity.

Melanin synthesis may be partly controlled by *melanocyte-stimulating hormone* (MSH) secreted by the pituitary gland beneath the mid-brain in the bony roof of the mouth. Diseases such as Addison's disease causing undersecretion of adrenocortical *hormones* may also increase melanin synthesis. The urine is darkened by excretion of the pigment.

Albinism is the absence of melanin from body tissues. It is caused by a genetic error (see *deoxyribonucleic acid*) leading to the failure of cells to synthesize the second enzyme, O-diphenol oxidase, involved in conversion of tyrosine to melanin.

Melanocyte-stimulating hormone (MSH)

A *hormone* secreted by the pituitary gland below the mid-brain in the roof of the mouth which stimulates skin cells, melanocytes, to synthesize and secrete *melanin*. Melanin is a pigment found in hair, nipples, the aureoles of breasts and the anus and in tanning. Black or brown people have more skin melanin than white people.

In animals, the hormone is secreted by an intermediate segment of the pituitary which does not exist in humans. There is some doubt, therefore, whether humans secrete MSH, but a sequence of *amino acids* identical to those in monkey MSH has been identified in human anterior or forward pituitary cells. Both *adrenocorticotropic hormone* and *testosterone* can cause skin cells to darken, however, and it is possible that they are acting like MSH in humans.

MSH is a polypeptide, that is, a chain of *amino acids* which is too small to be considered a *protein*.

Melatonin

A *hormone* secreted by cells in the pineal body. The pineal is a structure near the topological centre of the human brain. Its role in humans is unknown, nor has any function for melatonin been discovered.

In birds and possibly in rats, the pineal appears to be a regulator of the oestrus, a response that may be controlled by light. This interesting connection could explain the ancient notion that the pineal is a third eye, but if that is the case, it suggests that medieval physicians and philosophers possessed unsuspected anatomical sophistication.

In any case, melatonin is a breakdown product of the *transmitter, serotonin*. Its structural formula is:

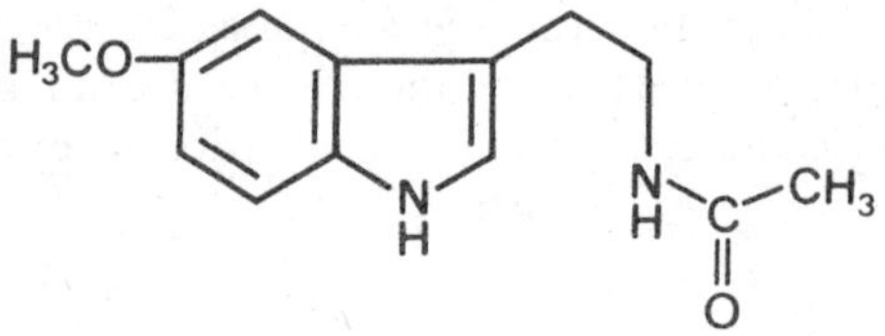

Milk

Fluid excreted by mammary glands forming the natural food of all young mammals. The process of milk secretion is called lactation.

Milk is a good source of most of the essential elements of the diet. A comparison of human and cow's milk shows some important differences in content, however. The figures in the table on p. 129 are based on 200 ml or about half a pint.

Note that the relatively large amount of phosphorus in cow's milk may impair the intake of calcium and magnesium by human infants. If this happens, nerve cells are adversely affected and the infant may suffer from convul-

	Human	Cow (pasteurized)
Energy (kCal)	150	130
Proteins (gm)	2	7
Carbohydrate (mostly *lactose*) (gm)	14	10
Fat (gm)	9	7
Cholesterol (mg)	30	30
Calcium (mg)	60	240
Phosphorus (mg)	30	195
Potassium (mg)	100	320
Sodium (mg)	35	100
Magnesium (mg)	20	30
Iron (mg)	.1	.16
Vitamin		
A (microgm equiv.)	120	80
D (microgm equiv.)	Depends on mother's intake	.06
C (microgm equiv.)	Depends on mother's intake	1
E (alpha-tocopherol, microgm equiv.)	.5	.2
B_1 (microgm equiv.)	.03	.08
B_2 (microgm equiv.)	.08	.3
B_3 (microgm equiv.)	1	1.8
B_6 (microgm equiv.)	.04	.08
Pantothenic acid (microgm equiv.)	.5	.7
Folic acid (microgm equiv.)	5	7
Biotin (microgm equiv.)	.4	4
B_{12} (microgm equiv.)	.2	.8

Adapted from S. Bingham, *Nutrition* (London: Corgi, 1978), p. 216

sions. Cow's milk protein may also be antigenic (see *antigen*) in some human infants. It is thought possible that an extreme allergy-like reaction against cow's milk protein could be the cause of cot death, a tragedy that is more common amongst bottle-fed than breast-fed babies. Although the vitamin content of human milk is lower than that of cow's milk, it is adequate to meet infant needs. The higher energy value of human milk is related to its greater carbohydrate and fat content.

The vitamins C and D in human milk depend on the mother's diet, but other substances will be drawn from her tissues for a few days if her diet is inadequate. If a poor diet continues, milk secretion gradually dries up. Anxiety and depression can also inhibit milk production, probably because these disorders affect nerve cells in the hypothalamus, a mid-brain centre with some influence over the emotions. The hypothalamus also contains nerve cells which secrete *releasing factors* that cause the secretion of pituitary *hormones* such as *prolactin*.

Milk is secreted by cells lining the alveoli or hollows within the mammary gland. The glands occur in both sexes, but the alveoli and secretory cells develop under the influence of the female hormones, *oestrogen* and *progesterone*. Oestrogen production during the first half of the menstrual cycle causes slight breast enlargement, but full development occurs only during pregnancy under the influence of prolactin. Although prolactin secretion is a response to a rising *blood* level of oestrogen, high doses of oestrogen and progesterone given for medical reasons during pregnancy can inhibit both breast development and lactation. The mechanism of this apparently contradictory action is unclear, but its importance is underlined by the fact that oestrogen and progesterone may be given to control later stages of breast cancer despite the customary removal of the ovaries which is usually an early form of therapy.

Suckling initiates milk release by stimulating pituitary secretion of several hormones: *oxytocin* and *vasopressin* by the posterior portion of the gland and *adrenocorticotropic hormone* as well as prolactin by the anterior pituitary. Suckling may also stimulate milk release directly through nervous connections between the teat and alveolar tissue. Milk pressure increases very soon after suckling begins, implying a direct nervous mechanism. Cessation of milk secretion probably reflects both emotional circumstances and the gradual change in hormonal output after birth.

Minerals

Homogeneous, non-organic elements which must be supplied as nutrients. They form body structures such as *bone*, and are required in *coenzymes* and as *electrolytes*.

The minerals needed by the body are listed in *body elements*. The eight found in the largest quantity are *calcium, chlorine, iron, magnesium, phosporous, potassium, sodium* and *sulphur*.

Monoamine oxidase (MAO)

An *enzyme* which catalyzes the breakdown of monoamines; that is, chemicals containing a single amine group (see *amino acid) such as adrenaline, noradrenaline* and *serotonin*. The latter two are *transmitters* of signals between nerve cells or neurons, and the enzyme acts in the space between neurons, the synaptic gap, as well as inside neurons to inactivate monoamines. MAO also acts in the gut and liver to catalyze the breakdown of tyramine, a monoamine found in many cheeses, Marmite, beer and red wine.

During the 1950s, doctors using a drug, iproniazid, to treat tuberculosis discovered that it also improved the mood of patients who were depressed, often because of their illness. The drug inhibits MAO. It was thought that it improved mood because it contributes to the excited state of some neurons by perpetuating the excitatory transmitters, noradrenaline and serotonin. The evidence is good that the period of transmitter activity is lengthened by the drug, but the relationship between transmitter activity and emotional normality or depression is complex. Indeed, MAO inhibitor drugs exert other effects on neurons, and mood improvement may have nothing to do with their inhibition of the enzyme. Nevertheless, patients using MAO inhibitor drugs must avoid tyramine-containing foods. If the enzyme is partially inactivated so that tyramine enters the *blood*, it causes noradrenaline release by *adrenergic* neurons. The effect may be high blood pressure, severe headache and in extreme cases, a fatal stroke or heart attack.

Mucus

A clear, viscous fluid consisting of *sugars* and a *protein* called mucin. Mucin is also found in *saliva*. Mucus forms a

131

protective coating on membrane surfaces, especially the lining of the stomach. It is synthesized by mucosal cells in the stomach lining, the mouth, nose and vagina.

Myelin

A fatty substance surrounding all large axons, the nerve cell (or neuron) processes which conduct a signal away from the cell body to the next neuron (see *sodium*).

Myelin is synthesized by Schwann cells (Theodor Schwann, German physiologist, 1810–82) which enwrap all neurons. The myelin coat isolates the axon from the *body fluids* and speeds up nerve signals. Small axons in the brain and peripheral nervous system are not myelinated and transmit signals more slowly. Myelin is laid down in concentric rings forming a tree-trunk like structure around the axon. It maintains roughly the same thickness through-out life unless it is damaged or destroyed by an accident or by a disease such as multiple sclerosis.

In multiple sclerosis, the myelin sheath disappears from axons, usually in a limited region in the brain, spinal cord or at the periphery. Without myelin, these cells can no longer signal. The lost myelin cannot be replaced. Attacks are not always repeated, but if they are, new groups of neurons are damaged and any disability spreads. If the attacks continue, the disease may be fatal. Its cause is unknown.

Myosin

An *enzyme, adenosine triphosphatase* (ATPase; see *adenosine triphosphate* (ATP)) in all muscle cells forming part of the contracting mechanism.

Myosin was first observed in the fibres of striated mus-cles, the voluntary skeletal muscles of the arms, legs, trunk and neck. Each muscle fibre consists of several myofibrils (Gr.: *mys* = muscle) where the characteristic striations originate. Under the light microscope, the striations resolve into bands, zones and lines as in the diagram:

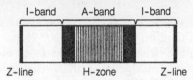

When the muscle contracts, the I-bands and the H-zone shorten, but the A-band remains constant in size. Thus, the darkest portions of the A-band on either side of the H-zone enlarge.

The striations reflect the arrangement of myosin in combination with a smaller *protein*, actin, in the myofibril. Each myofibril contains seven myosin molecules and six actin molecules arranged in a honeycomb:

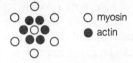

Looked at sideways rather than head on, the myosin and actin are arranged so that cross-bridges from the myosin cause it to pull the actin along during contraction. The nature of the cross-bridges is not clear, but *magnesium ions* are required to make them work. Each cross-bridge releases the actin and reattaches to it in a coordinated manner like a ratchet mechanism.

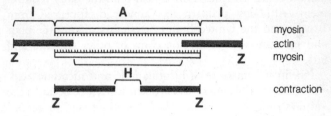

The myosin pulls the actin inwards, shortening the myofibril. *Calcium* ions must also be present in the inter-cellular fluid if the protein is to act. It then catalyzes the separation of a phosphate group from ATP, releasing the energy stored in the bond. Some of the ADP thus formed is re-energized by the addition of a phosphate group supplied by another energy-rich molecule, creatine phosphate, but the larger part of the new ATP is probably derived from the operation of the *citric acid* cycle. About 25 per cent of the energy obtained from ATP in muscle is converted by actin-myosin into mechanical activity; that is, contraction. The remainder is dissipated as heat. In other words, muscle has a maximum efficiency of 25 per cent.

Niacin (Nicotinamide, Nicotinic acid)

Vitamin B_3, though this designation is more common in the United States than in the United Kingdom. Niacin deficiency causes pellagra. The symptoms include skin sores, diarrhoea, a sore and swollen tongue and mental disturbances akin to dementia. Unless the *vitamin* deficiency is corrected, the patient will die. Even after the patient is out of danger, it may be necessary to treat other deficiencies that have arisen because of the disease before full health can be restored.

Niacin is widely available in food. It is not destroyed by standing or by cooking. Though it is leeched out of meats and vegetables by boiling, it can be recovered if the water is used to make soup. The best sources of niacin are beef extract, fried liver and peanuts. Even a cup of ground or instant coffee provides more niacin than the daily requirement. Although pellagra has almost disappeared from Britain and the United States, it persists among the poor and ignorant who subsist on chips or other starches and fats.

Niacin is a mixture of nicotinamide and nicotinic acid. The former is harmless when taken in excess because the kidneys filter it out of the *blood*. Nicotinic acid in excess, however, may cause flushing and a burning sensation. It is chemically related to the nicotine in tobacco, but has different physiological effects. Some nicotinic acid is synthesized by human cells from the *amino acid*, tryptophan, but not enough to supply the body's needs. Nicotinic acid is converted to nicotinamide, and this substance is used by cells to synthesize the important *coenzyme, nicotinamide adenine dinucleotide* (NAD). NAD plays a major role in energy formation and storage, both in the *citric acid* cycle and in the electron transport process (see *cytochrome*) which produces *adenosine triphosphate*. The symptoms of pellagra arise because without NAD, the body's energy supplies are impaired and many enzymes malfunction.

Nicotinamide adenine dinucleotide (NAD)

A *coenzyme* required by *enzymes* engaged in the detoxification of ethyl alcohol (see *alcohol dehydrogenase*), the biosynthesis of fatty acids (see *fat, lipid*) and the formation and storage of energy. A chemically similar coenzyme, nicotinamide adenine dinucleotide phosphate (NADP), is required for the synthesis of fatty acids, *steroids* and the nucleic acids, *deoxyribonucleic acid* and *ribonucleic acid*.

NAD was the first coenzyme to be discovered. It was isolated from yeast in 1904 and was described chemically thirty years later.

Both NAD and NADP are the sites of oxidation-reduction reactions. They accept *hydrogen* removed from a compound such as ethyl alcohol and release it, often to combine with *oxygen* to form water. In the *citric acid* cycle and the electron transport process (see *cytochrome*) leading to the formation of another coenzyme, *adenosine triphosphate*, NAD and NADP play this vital role without which energy can be neither created nor stored.

The NAD molecule consists of two *nucleotides* linked by the two phosphates. One nucleotide contains *adenine* and the other, nicotinamide, derived from *niacin*. In NADP, there is an additional phosphate group. The hydrogen is accepted and released by the nicotinamide portion of the molecule, but it can act only in combination with the adenine nucleotide and the phosphates because of the electrochemical forces existing in the whole molecule.

Nitrogen (N)

A colourless gas, the fourth most common element in the

body. Nitrogen is a constituent of all *amino acids* and therefore, of all *proteins*.

Carbohydrates and *fats* contain no nitrogen, but it is obtained from any proteinaceous food as part of the amino acids. Although nitrogen makes up about four-fifths of the atmosphere, the gas cannot be used physiologically unless it is first formed into amino acids, a process which can be performed by nitrogen-fixing bacteria and plants such as peas and alfalfa but not by animal body cells.

Indeed, if it is breathed alone without *oxygen*, atmospheric nitrogen can be a poison. It is soluble in *blood* plasma and other *body fluids*. If air is breathed under pressure as it is by divers, more nitrogen is absorbed. If the pressure is suddenly reduced, dissolved nitrogen is released as bubbles which block blood vessels causing the pain of the bends. Even at normal atmospheric pressure, however, nitrogen dissolved in body fluids can be troublesome.

A healthy person is said to be in nitrogen balance; that is, nitrogen intake is equal to nitrogen loss. Although it is absorbed as amino acids, nitrogen is excreted principally as *urea* in urine. Additional nitrogen loss occurs because of the rubbing away of skin, the growth of nails and hair and in *sweat*. Altogether an adult requires about two grams of nitrogen a day. Growing children and pregnant women must have more to maintain a balance because they are using protein to build new tissues.

The nitrogen-fixation process is essentially ammonia synthesis, or in other words, the reduction of nitrogen by the addition of *hydrogen*. The energy required by the process, which involves several steps, is obtained from sunlight acting through pigments such as chlorophyll. The ammonia is used to synthesize amino acids.

Nitrogen has atomic number 7. Its atomic weight is 14.007.

Noradrenaline (US: Norepinephrine)

A *transmitter* of signals between some nerve cells or neurons in the brain and spinal cord, between neurons and small arteries, between neurons and the involuntary muscles of the intestinal walls and the eyes and between neurons and heart muscle. All such neurons are *adrenergic*; i.e., energized by noradrenaline.

Noradrenaline is also the chemical from which cells in the medullae or cores of the adrenal glands on top of the kidneys synthesize *adrenaline*. Only one step is required, the addition of one *carbon* and one *hydrogen* atom. The two chemicals are very similar in structure and, indeed, in function. In part, the effects of adrenaline probably reflect its action on adrenergic nerve and muscle cells.

The *receptors* for noradrenaline in muscle cells fall into two classes identified as alpha and beta. The alpha receptors are excitatory; that is, when they are bonded to noradrenaline, they cause the cell to contract (or if the muscle is normally held in a state of contraction as in a sphincter, excitation causes it to relax). Beta-receptors, on the other hand, inhibit the contraction of muscles excepting in the heart where beta receptors cause excitation. The two classes are defined on the basis of whether they cause excitation or inhibition in muscle cells in response to adrenaline. It is now customary, however, to designate heart muscle adrenergic receptors beta 1, and other smooth-muscle receptors, beta 2, thus avoiding the apparent contradiction. A further subdivision of alpha receptors into alpha 1 and alpha 2 has also been introduced. Alpha 2 receptors are found in the membranes of the neurons releasing noradrenaline. When they are excited by the transmitter, further emission of noradrenaline stops, another example of a negative feedback mechanism often seen in the regulation of *hormone* secretion.

There may also be a relationship between the release of noradrenaline by neurons and the presence of the local hormone, *prostaglandin*. Prostaglandin inhibits noradrenaline output, and it may have a regulatory role in the sympathetic nervous system (see *transmitter*).

Because it is an excitatory transmitter in brain regions that regulate emotions, noradrenaline has been implicated in mood. It is thought to be one of the chemical determinants of excitement or depression, for example. The *monoamine oxidase* inhibitor drugs used to control depression in some patients act in part by increasing the supplies of noradrenaline. However, the drugs also increase the amount of *serotonin*, another excitatory transmitter in the brain, and they may have other effects.

Noradrenaline is a catecholamine like adrenaline, *dopa* and *dopamine*. Its structural formula is:

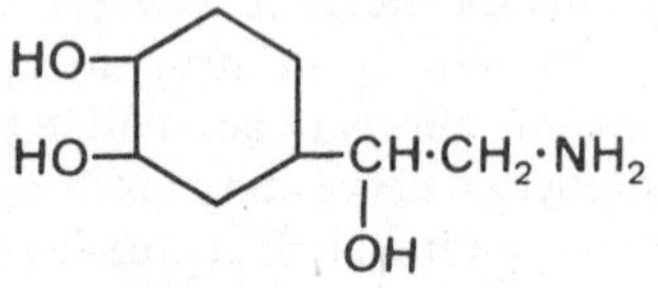
HO
HO
CH·CH2·NH2
OH

Nucleic acid (see *Deoxyribonucleic acid, Ribonucleic acid*)

Nucleotide

A molecule consisting of a *sugar, ribose*, linking a *base* and a phosphate (see *phosphorus*). The word is a reference to the nucleic acids which are made up from these molecules linked in long chains ribose to ribose via the phosphates, thus:

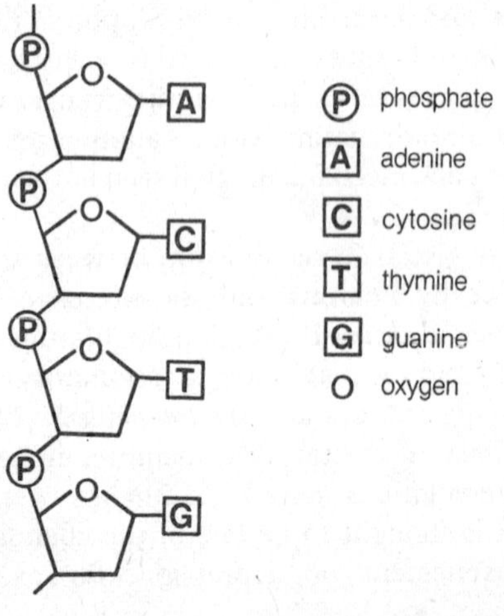
P
O
A
C
T
G
P phosphate
A adenine
C cytosine
T thymine
G guanine
O oxygen

The sequence in the diagram could form part of a *deoxyribonucleic acid* (DNA) molecule. The phosphate linkage involves a regular shift in the plane in which the sugar lies, accounting for the helical spiral of the nucleic acid.

Many *coenzymes* are also nucleotides. See *adenosine triphosphate*.

Oestrogen

One of the female *hormones* synthesized both in the ovaries and by cells in the cortex of the adrenal glands on top of the kidneys. The most active natural form is oestradiol.

Physiologically, the earliest effects of oestrogen are the changes in girls at puberty. They include breast development, pigmentation of the nipples and their surrounding aureoles, enlargement of the uterus and female distribution of body hair. The hormone contributes to body shape by affecting the growth of long *bones*.

After puberty and until menopause, oestrogen is produced by the ovaries during the first half of the monthly cycle. Its role is to prepare the body for conception. It may increase libido, but this effect is also attributed to secretion by the female adrenal cortex of the male hormone, *testosterone*. Oestrogen causes changes in the *mucous* lining of the vagina which facilitates sperm movement, prepares the uterus for implantation of a fertilized egg and possibly also produces a pheromone or natural body odour attractive to men. During pregnancy, oestrogen contributes to the further enlargement of the breasts and to the general feeling of well-being experienced by most women.

After menopause, ovarian synthesis of oestrogen falls sharply. Without replacement therapy using either oestrogen-like drugs or chemicals with similar effects, women will suffer from various unpleasant symptoms including hot flushes, vaginal dryness and a tendency to overweight. An oestrogen-containing contraceptive pill is most commonly prescribed.

Oestrogen is secreted by the adrenal cortex in men as well as women, but its role in the male body is unclear.

139

Either natural oestrogens, a related chemical or one which is unrelated but has similar effects may be useful in the treatment of prostatic cancer in men. It acts both by counteracting the growth-stimulation of testosterone and by depressing the pituitary gland control of male hormone production.

The role of oestrogen in the treatment of breast cancer is less easy to explain. The first form of therapy is often removal of the ovaries, presumably in part because oestrogen is stimulating cancer growth. Yet oestrogen or chemically different drugs with oestrogen-like activity may prove effective in the control of cancer growth later in the course of the disease. The reason for this apparent contradiction is not clear. It could reflect either a change in the sensitivity of the cancer cells to oestrogen or a change in some aspect of their environment or structure which alters the effect of the hormone.

Perhaps the most common use of oestrogen as a drug is in the oral contraceptive pill. The hormone or a similar chemical is combined with a *progesterone*-like substance. However, oestrogen has been implicated in *blood* clot formation both in women using the pill and in men given an oestrogen-like drug to control prostatic cancer. The newer oral contraceptives contain less oestrogen or none at all.

Oestrogen is secreted in the uterus by cells in the egg-producing follicles during the first two weeks of the oestral cycle before the egg is actually released. Follicular growth is stimulated by *follicle-stimulating hormone* (FSH) secreted by the anterior or forward portion of the pituitary in response to a *releasing factor* synthesized by nerve cells in the hypothalamus, a part of the mid-brain to which the pituitary is attached. Low *blood* levels of oestrogen stimulate secretion of FSH-releasing factor, and rising blood levels turn off the responsible hypothalamic nerve cells.

Oestrogen is a *steroid* synthesized from *cholesterol*. In fact, several steroids with oestrogen-like activity are synthesized naturally, the most active being oestradiol, as noted above. In its target cells, the hormone may stimulate ribonucleic acid (see *deoxyribonucleic acid, ribonucleic acid*) synthesis followed by manufacture of new *proteins*.

Oestrogen also stimulates an *enzyme* which enhances the utilization of *hydrogen* and *oxygen* by cells, but the relationship between these molecular effects and its physiological activity is not clear.

Opiate, natural (see *Endorphin*)

Oxygen (O)

(Gr.: *oxys* = sour + *gennan* = to produce)

A colourless, odourless gas, a constituent of most organic compounds and of water. Oxygen makes up about 20 per cent of the atmosphere. Excepting anaerobic bacteria which multiply only in the absence of oxygen, all forms of life require it. In sunlight, green plants and some bacteria respire oxygen obtained from *carbon dioxide*, the *carbon* having been used to synthesize *carbohydrates*. Animal cells break down carbohydrates in the presence of oxygen releasing the energy which may be stored for future use (see *citric acid, cytochrome*). Muscle can function for a short time in the absence of oxygen, but the energy produced is inadequate to maintain activity for very long.

Oxygen is used medically with general anaesthetics to protect the patient against oxygen shortage. It may also be used to supply additional needs, for example, during childbirth or when breathing is impaired by disease such as bronchitis or in heart failure. When circulation is poor, however, the value of pure oxygen is limited because tissue perfusion by the *blood* may be inadequate. Under pressure, oxygen may hasten recovery from shock and promote healing. It is used to treat infections caused by anaerobic bacteria such as tetanus.

The gas enters the blood in the alveoli, the tiny sacks of the lungs. It is taken up by *haemoglobin* and is released to all tissues through the smallest blood vessels, the capillaries, because the oxygen pressure in the tissues is lower than that in the blood.

Excessive breathing or hyperventilation may be toxic

because it can increase blood alkalinity abnormally, a condition called respiratory alkalosis (see also *acid, base*). The central factor in the onset of this condition is a relative fall in the blood level of carbon dioxide due to the increased oxygen being carried. The CO_2 decline causes a concomitant fall in the amount of bicarbonate which leads in turn to a slight relative decline in *carbonic acid* with a rise in pH (see Appendix 2). Normally, respiratory alkalosis is quickly overcome by reflex changes in breathing that stop hyperventilation, but under conditions of stress or poisoning, a more serious form of alkalosis may follow in which the red blood cells and kidneys also malfunction. Metabolic alkalosis, a condition brought on by the chemical activity or metabolism of cells throughout the body is much harder to correct. Indeed, it can be fatal. Metabolic alkalosis may originate with some abnormality other than hyperventilation and at the outset may have nothing to do with oxygen intake.

Oxygen can cause pain and even death if it is injected because it can form bubbles that block blood vessels. Such an accident can occur if a hypodermic needle is not properly evacuated before use.

Excepting for atmospheric oxygen, the gas is useful to the body only if it has previously become an element in organic compounds. The bubbles in oxygenated drinks, for example, escape from the stomach as a belch. Atmospheric oxygen is actually a molecule containing two atoms of oxygen, O_2. Ozone is O_3.

Oxygen is atomic number 5 and has atomic weight 15.999.

Oxytocin

(Gr.: *oxys* = sharp, sour + *tokos* = birth)

A *hormone* secreted by the posterior portion of the pituitary gland in the roof of the mouth beneath the mid-brain. Oxytocin stimulates involuntary muscle in the breast, gut and uterus causing it to contract. As the name implies, its primary role is to cause contractions of the parturient uterus.

One other hormone, *vasopressin*, is also secreted by the posterior pituitary. Oxytocin and vasopressin may both be synthesized by cells in the hypothalamus, that portion of the mid-brain to which the pituitary is connected. The hormones are thought to travel via the connecting nerve cells into the posterior pituitary. The two hormones are very similar structurally. Both are nonapeptides; that is, a chain of nine *amino acids* with differences in the third and the eighth:

$$S \text{——————} S$$
Oxytocin   Cy—Tyr—Ile—Gln—Asn—Cy—Pro—Leu—Gly—NH$_2$

$$S \text{——————} S$$
Vasopressin   Cy—Tyr—Phe—Gln—Asn—Cy—Pro—Arg—Gly—NH$_2$

Cy = cysteine	Asn = asparagine
Tyr = tyrosine	Pro = proline
Ile = isoleucine	Leu = leucine
Gln = glutamine	Phe = phenylalanine
Gly = glycine	Arg = arginine

The hormone regulates the periodicity of contractions. After childbirth, it causes milk ejection. Oxytocin or a synthetic substitute may be used to induce labour. Its effect in the uterus is probably a consequence of the release of *calcium ions* by muscle cells, but the precise mechanism of action is not known.

Parathormone (Parathyroid hormone)

A *hormone* secreted by the parathyroid gland behind the thyroid at the top of the thorax and in the base of the neck. With calcitonin and *vitamin* D, parathormone regulates amounts of *calcium* in the *blood*. If calcium levels fall, the parathyroid secretes the hormone, increasing blood calcium from three sources: reabsorption from urine by cells lining the kidney tubules, increased absorption from food through the small intestine and resorption from *bone*. Because bone calcium is associated with *phosphorus*, blood levels of phosphate *ions* also rise under the influence of the hormone.

Parathormone secretion is regulated directly by the blood level of calcium. Excess parathormone may be secreted if the parathyroid gland grows too large or if it is invaded by a tumour. This condition, known as hyperparathyroidism, can cause kidney stones which are precipitated because the blood contains abnormally large amounts of calcium. Ultimately, kidney damage will occur with an increase in urine volume followed by dehydration. Other signs of hyperparathyroidism include mental disorder, weakness and bone brittleness leading to fractures. Surgery to remove part of the gland or the tumour is usually an effective treatment.

The opposite condition, hypoparathyroidism, can be more acute. Calcium deficiency accompanied by phosphate deficiency causes increased nervous excitability because the nerve cells tend to signal with less stimulation as a result of the relative absence of calcium from the fluids surrounding the cells. Excitability may cause uncontrolled muscular contraction, tetany, including contraction of the entrance to the windpipe with danger of choking. Colic-like gut pains, breathing difficulties arising from constriction of the air passages in the lungs and sweating may also occur. Hypoparathyroidism is clearly dangerous and must be quickly dealt with by injecting calcium and vitamin D as well as parathormone. Because the hormone causes bone resorption, maintenance therapy for hypoparathyroidism requires continuous dietary supplements of calcium and vitamin D.

Ultimately, of course, all calcium comes from food, but the most important source of the mineral in response to hormone secretion is bone. The hormone stimulates an *enzyme, adenyl cyclase*, to produce *cyclic adenosine monophosphate* (cAMP). What happens next is not clear, but the cAMP probably causes the transfer of phosphates to intracellular organelles which are involved in calcium release from bone.

Parathormone is a polypeptide with 84 *amino acids*, of which the first 34 have the activity of the whole molecule.

Pepsin

(Gr.: *pepsis* = digestion)

An *enzyme* produced by cells in the stomach wall. It is responsible for the first step in *protein* digestion. Later protein breakdown is accomplished by *chymotrypsin* and *trypsin*, enzymes secreted by the pancreas, and erepsin from the small intestine.

Pepsin is secreted in the form of a larger molecule, pepsinogen. In the presence of *hydrochloric acid*, pepsinogen is broken down to form pepsin. Secretion takes place in response to food in the stomach and brain stimulation of the principal nerve affecting the stomach, the vagus.

The enzyme consists of four slightly different molecules. Pepsin I comes from pepsinogen I which is secreted by cells throughout the stomach wall. Pepsins II, IIa and III derive from pepsinogens II and III which are secreted by cells at the top of the stomach. All four pepsins split proteins at the *nitrogen* terminals of two *amino acids*, phenylalanine and tyrosine.

Peptide

A compound consisting of two or more *amino acids* joined by reaction of the *nitrogen*-containing amide (NH_2) and carboxyl (COOH) groups on adjacent amino acids. Such a reaction forms a peptide bond or peptide linkage. It is formed by the loss of one *hydrogen* atom from the amide and one *oxygen* and one hydrogen from the carboxyl; that is, by the removal of water leaving CO·NH.

Polypeptides are molecules consisting of three or more amino acids. *Oxytocin* and *vasopressin*, for example, are both polypeptide *hormones* containing nine amino acids.

Perspiration (see *Sweat*)

Phenylalanine (see *Amino acid, Pepsin*)

Phosphorus

(P) (Gr.: *phos* = light + *phorein* = to carry)

A non-metallic element, poisonous and inflammable, found in living matter bound to four *oxygen* atoms as phosphate. The body contains about 600 grams of phosphorus (just under a pound), about 80 per cent of which combines with *calcium* as apatite to form *bone* and in a slightly different compound, tooth *dentine*. The remainder is found in cells in nucleic acids (see *deoxyribonucleic acid, ribonucleic acid*), energy-storage compounds (see *adenosine triphosphate*), coenzymes such as *nicotinamide adenine dinucleotide*, and in the *myelin* sheath surrounding the long processes of some nerve cells.

Phosphorus is found in all foods except *fat, sugar* and alcohol. The best sources – *milk*, cheese, meat, fish and eggs – also contain calcium and *proteins*. In cereals, nuts and pulses, phosphorus occurs in the form of phytic acid which forms insoluble compounds with calcium and *iron* so that the phosphorus is not available for use by body cells. In wheat bread, however, an *enzyme*, phytase, breaks down phytic acid during proving so that the phosphates can be absorbed. All normal diets supply adequate amounts for healthy people. Though they may be harmless, phosphorus-containing tonics are of doubtful value.

A phosphate deficiency with potentially dangerous results can arise out of excessive use of some antacids. These drugs bind food phosphates, preventing their entry into the *blood*. Phosphorus needs are then supplied by removing phosphate from bone. Unless the antacid is discontinued, weakness, pain and loss of appetite can ensue leading eventually to coma and death.

Plasmin (see *Blood factor*)

Porphyrin

A class of molecules of which the haem of *haemoglobin* is the most familiar. All human porphyrins contain an atom of *iron* at the centre of each molecule. However, the analogous corrin nucleus in *cyanocobalamin, vitamin* B_{12}, contains cobalt. In green plants, the porphyrin in chlorophyll contains an atom of magnesium, and other porphyrins have at their centres atoms of zinc, nickel, *copper* and even silver.

All porphyrins consist of four pyrrole nuclei. A diagram of the porphyrin molecule is given in the entry on haemoglobin. It is synthesized by cells in *bone* marrow, spleen and probably other tissues from acetate, a *carbohydrate*, and the *amino acid, glycine*. The parent substance, porphin, gives rise to several slightly different porphyrins. For example, haem is a member of the group called protoporphyrin.

Urine normally contains small amounts of porphyrins excreted from the breakdown of haem, the *cytochromes* or similar molecules. Excess porphyrin excretion may be a sign of a disease, one of a class known as porphyria. Many such disorders are inherited. In one, the most prominent symptom is extreme skin sensitivity. In another, skin disorder is accompanied by abdominal pain and mental confusion which comes and goes unpredictably. It is thought that George III's madness may have been caused by this form of porphyria. It is almost certainly inherited.

Potassium (K) (L.: *kalium*)

A metallic element required for the proper functioning of nerve and muscle cells.

Adults contain 100 to 150 grams (3½ to 5 ounces) of potassium and lose between half and one gram a day excreted in the urine. Losses must be made up from food. Except *fat, sugar* and alcohol, all foods contain potassium, but dried fruits, nuts, wholemeal bread and instant coffee are rich sources.

Potassium *ions* in nerve and muscle cells contribute to their excitability by moving into the tissue fluid in partial exchange for *sodium* ions in the fluid. The interiors of these cells are normally electrically negative in relation to the fluid surrounding them, a condition maintained chiefly because the cell membranes exclude sodium. Excitation begins with a change in the cell membrane which permits a sudden inflow of sodium. Because the sodium is a positively charged ion, moreover, an electrochemical current is established across the cell membrane. Shortly after the inflow of sodium ions begins, potassium, also a positive ion, flows more slowly out of the cell marking the beginning of the recovery phase during which the electrochemical current stops and sodium ions are actually pumped out of the cell returning the interior to a negative potential. Meanwhile, in a nerve cell, the movement of ions has continued further along the cell carrying the signal towards the cell's extremity. Because the electrochemical excitation is a response to potential difference between the inside and the outside of the cell, the excitation itself is called an action potential. For a more detailed description, see *sodium*.

Diarrhoea, drugs that increase urine output and some anti-cancer drugs can cause pronounced potassium loss. The elderly are particularly prone to such a malfunction. It can lead to weakness, mental confusion, kidney damage and in extreme cases, a heart attack. The best antidote is potassium-rich food.

Progesterone

One of the female *hormones*, synthesized both in the ovaries and in the cortex of the adrenal glands on top of the kidneys. Progesterone causes changes to take place in the uterus that prepare it for implantation of a fertilized egg. If pregnancy occurs, progesterone is produced by the ovaries until the placenta itself begins to secrete the hormone after about three months. Progesterone prevents further menstruation and ovulation. It is this capacity to inhibit ovulation that is the basis for the use of progesterone-like chemicals in the contraceptive pill.

Progesterone is secreted by the cells of the egg-producing follicle in the second half of the menstrual cycle. During the first two weeks, before the egg is released, the same cells produce *oestrogen*. After release, the cells change their appearance as well as their function. They enlarge and are filled with *fat* which gives them a yellowish colour, the origin of the name, corpus luteum or yellow body.

If pregnancy does not occur, progesterone secretion declines from about the twenty-sixth day. Without hormonal support, the prepared lining of the uterus breaks up and is eliminated in the menstrual flow.

Progesterone secretion is indirectly regulated by the anterior or forward pituitary gland which is under the control of the hypothalamus, that portion of the mid-brain to which the pituitary is attached. The shift in ovarian follicular function takes place in response to the secretion of *luteinizing hormone* (LH) by the pituitary in response to LH-*releasing factor* from hypothalamic nerve cells. LH-releasing factor is secreted in response to a low *blood* level of progesterone and stops when the blood level of progesterone rises towards the end of the menstrual cycle.

Progesterone may perform physiological functions apart from the maintenance of pregnancy. It has been used as a drug to combat both cancer of the uterus and breast cancer. In men, it may help in the treatment of prostate cancer, against which oestrogen may also be useful. In light of these therapeutic applications, it is thought that the hormone may play some general protective role.

Progesterone is a *steroid* closely related chemically to oestrogen and the male hormone, *testosterone*. It is the most active of a group of naturally occurring chemicals, the progestins. Its mechanism of action in the cell is not understood.

Prolactin

A female *hormone* secreted by the anterior or forward pituitary gland in the bony roof of the mouth directly below the mid-brain of which it is a part. Prolactin stimulates breast development and lactation. Until recently, there has been doubt that prolactin differed from human *growth hormone*, but its independent status is now established in all mammals.

After childbirth, loss of the female hormone, *oestrogen*,

from the placenta stimulates prolactin output. Indeed, even in non-pregnant women, stroking the breast and nipple can stimulate prolactin production. Breast tissue has already been prepared by the high *blood* level of the other female hormone, *progesterone*, which has been maintained throughout pregnancy. In response to the prolactin and to suckling, lactation commences. Yet both progesterone and high oestrogen levels may inhibit prolactin release and lactation. There is no explanation for this apparent contradiction, but it is not the only one revealed by the female hormones. It seems probable that both the timing of their output and the status of their target cells plays a role in hormone action.

There is also evidence that *dopamine*, a mid-brain transmitter of signals between nerve cells, inhibits prolactin secretion.

Prolactin is now the only anterior pituitary hormone for which no *releasing factor* has been discovered. Cells in the hypothalamus, the mid-brain region to which the pituitary is attached, secrete several chemicals which cause the anterior pituitary to secrete its other hormones. Prolactin secretion seems to be self-regulating, another example of negative feedback. That is, the appearance of the substance in the blood inhibits secretion, and conversely, secretion is stimulated by a fall in blood level. It is also influenced, however, by the blood levels of the other female hormones.

Prolactin is a polypeptide consisting of 200 *amino acids*. Its mechanism of action is not understood.

Prostacyclin (see *Prostaglandin*)

Prostaglandin

One of a class of *hormones* secreted in various parts of the body with powerful effects on smooth muscles; that is, those not under voluntary control, in the uterus, prostate gland, seminal vesicles, *blood* vessels, lungs, gut and other tissues. Very little prostaglandin is needed to produce an effect. Because it is synthesized throughout the body and acts on cells immediately adjacent to those secreting it, prostaglandin is called a local hormone.

It was discovered by a Swedish biochemist, von Euler, in 1935. The name derives from the fact that it was first isolated from prostate gland tissue.

In the initiation and continuation of labour, prostaglandins may enhance the effect of the posterior pituitary hormone, *oxytocin*, and they have been used as drugs to start labour instead of oxytocin. In men, prostaglandin is the immediate cause of the contractions that produce ejaculation of seminal fluid. Prostaglandin mediates some pain sensation, at least in part because it causes the contraction of smooth muscle. It is one of the chemicals active in the inflammatory process, entering the cascade after *histamine* and the *leukotrienes*. Because it causes smooth muscle in the lungs to relax rather than contract, prostaglandin may help asthma patients. It also relaxes muscle cells in small blood vessels and can cause a fall in blood pressure.

Underlying these diverse effects are a variety of prostaglandins, all similar but each with slight atomic differences. The basic molecule is a fatty acid (see *lipid*) consisting of 20 *carbon* atoms of which numbers eight and twelve are bonded to form a structure roughly like this:

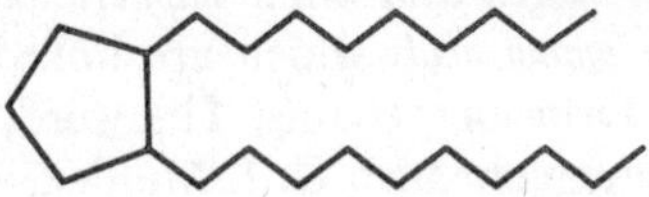

The chains contain at least one double bond, and the molecule is unsaturated. It is synthesized from arachidonic acid, the chemical which also gives rise to the leukotrienes. Thus, it is possible that aspirin relieves pain by inhibiting the *enzyme* that converts arachidonic acid to prostaglandin. A similar chemical, prostacyclin, inhibits blood-clot formation by slowing the aggregation of blood platelets.

The mechanism of action of the prostaglandins at the cellular level is not known. They release the enzyme, *adenyl cyclase*, in cells or cell membranes causing formation of *cyclic adenosine monophosphate* from *adenosine triphosphate*. Cyclic AMP has been called the second messenger carrying hormonal signals inside the target cells. On some smooth muscle cells, prostaglandins may act indirectly. They inhibit release from nerve cells of the *transmitter, noradrenaline,* which carries signals from the nerve cell to the smooth muscle cell. Thus, prostaglandin prevents excitation of the muscle cell.

Like other natural substances such as *endorphin, insulin* and *interferon,* there has been much interest in the use of prostaglandins as drugs apart from their use in obstetrics. They are quickly destroyed by an *enzyme,* ptyalin, *saliva* and gastric juices (see *hydrochloric acid, pepsin*) and cannot be given orally; in the body, enzymes quickly break them down. The side effects observed after their use as drugs include pain and diarrhoea and have so far made them counter productive.

Prosthetic group (see *Coenzyme*)

Protein

(Gr.: *protos* = first)

One of a very large class of compounds consisting of *carbon, hydrogen, nitrogen, oxygen* and often *sulphur.* These elements are formed into *amino acids* which are linked together by *peptide* bonds to form long chains. The word, protein, was first used by a Dutch chemist, G. J. Mulder, in 1838.

With *carbohydrate* and *fat,* protein is a major constituent of all organisms. It is found in all cells, either forming part of the cell structure or playing a functional role.

Structural proteins form part of the membrane surrounding cells and the intracellular organelles such as mitochondria, though it is probable that many function in the membranes as *enzymes.* Proteins also form a structural part of the chromosomes in cell nuclei. The principal extracellular structural proteins are *collagen* and *keratin.*

With the exception of enzymes in membranes, functional proteins have no role in body structures as such. They include *antibodies,* carrier proteins such as *cytochrome* and *haemoglobin,* several *hormones* and the thousands of enzymes which catalyze almost every one of the millions of chemical conversions of life.

The diversity and complexity of these roles is possible because proteins are huge molecules. They can be made up of several thousand amino acids and take many shapes. Each protein consists of thousands of atoms. Their attractive and repulsive forces cause the molecule to take up complicated forms. The chain of amino acids itself is linked by peptide bonds to form polypeptides of great length, the primary structure of a protein. The amino acids turn and twist with respect to each other in a secondary structure. This consists in part of a right-handed helix, analogous to the *deoxyribonucleic acid* (DNA) helix, and in part of straight sections. Because of the internal atomic forces, the secondary structure is further distorted until it may resemble a rubber band rolled back and forth between your hands. This form, which differs with each protein, is called the tertiary structure. Finally, several tertiary structures may come together to form a unit bound by weak bonds like hydrogen bonds. Haemoglobin contains two units of one protein and two of a second. Collagen is composed of regularly repeating units, but enzyme molecules consist of fantastic shapes which make them capable of performing catalytic activities. Combinations of tertiary structures are called quaternary.

The sequence of amino acids forming the protein determines its structure and thence its function. That sequence is dictated by the nucleic acids in the cells. The process by which DNA is transcribed into *ribonucleic acid* (RNA) and the translation of RNA into protein is relatively well understood. Much uncertainty still surrounds the selectivity of protein synthesis. If it is true that what we inherit through our genes is the capacity to make some proteins but not others (for example, blood type A but not blood type B; see *blood group*), then all the cells in your body with the exception of egg or sperm cells must contain the same protein-making ability. Yet nerve cells, for example, can transmit electrochemical signals and liver cells can detoxify alcohol because of the proteins they synthesize. The enzymes that make it possible for nerve cells to function differ from those in liver cells. They are not totally different packages of enzymes because all cells require energy, but they differ in respect to the enzymes that catalyze their unique functions. Why do cells in different tissues in the same body synthesize different enzymes? Although there is evidence for the existence of gene repressor chemicals and gene initiators, the complete picture cannot yet be drawn.

Nitrogen as part of amino acids, and the eight essential amino acids, must be supplied in the diet. All dietary proteins, excepting a few which may be antigenic to some people, are digested to their constituent amino acids, and it is these which are absorbed. Adults require between 38 and 45 grams of protein per day to make up for cell destruction and replace nitrogen losses. Growing children and pregnant women need about 10 per cent more, but such minimums are probably inadequate because diets which are so low in protein tend also to lack adequate *iron* and B *vitamins*. Protein requirements also increase during periods of physical or even psychic stress.

If the diet is poor in protein, the body draws on fats and carbohydrates to make up the deficit. In starvation, structural and muscle proteins are broken down and recycled to maintain the essential enzymes. In such extreme conditions, disease is common: in children, kwashiorkor and marasmus characterized by weakness and skin sores are eventually fatal.

Excess protein intake is no problem for adults. They can store the carbon, oxygen and hydrogen as carbohydrate or fat and excrete the potentially toxic nitrogen as *urea*. The kidneys of infants cannot yet cope with the urea, however, unless they are given much more water too. A diet containing excessive protein can permanently damage an infant's kidneys.

High protein diets cut down on the need for carbohydrates and fats because proteins can be converted for use as fuel. The conversion also requires energy and draws on fat. This may be desirable for overweight people, but it is an inefficient use of food resources.

The most concentrated food source, low-fat soya flour, contains about 50 per cent protein by weight. Meat, fish, cheese, eggs, most nuts and pulses are excellent sources. By and large, meat proteins including cheese, eggs and *milk* are more efficiently utilized because of their relatively high ratio of proteins to fats and carbohydrates. Vegetables contain more of other dietary essentials such as the B vitamins, however. For the normal person, a vegetarian diet is acceptable providing it includes the protein-rich nuts and pulses.

Pyridoxine (Pyridoxal, Pyridoxamine)

Vitamin B_6. Although no single disease analogous to pellagra (see *niacin*) is attributable to pyridoxine deficiency, serious symptoms including skin lesions, *blood* disorders and convulsions can be fatal in the total absence of the vitamin.

It has been shown to inhibit the aggregation of blood platelets and blood clotting, and it may prove useful in the prevention of thrombosis, a clot that blocks a blood vessel. The principal physiological role of the vitamin is to form a *coenzyme*, pyridoxal phosphate, required by *enzymes* catalyzing the recycling of *amino acids* for *protein* biosynthesis, and the synthesis of *nitrogen*-containing compounds such as *adrenaline, dopamine, gamma-amino butyric acid* (GABA), *histamine, noradrenaline* and *serotonin*. Convulsions occur because of inadequate or unbalanced supplies of the *transmitters* of signals between nerve cells, dopamine, GABA, noradrenaline and serotonin. Protein shortages impair growth and blood formation. Pyridoxal phosphate is also required by enzymes involved in the biosynthesis of *porphyrins*, a principal constituent of the haem molecule, a second cause of the blood disorders that result from pyridoxine deficiency.

All foods except *fat, sugar* and alcohol contain some vitamin B_6. The richest sources are yeast, liver, kidney, fish and meat. Like all B vitamins, pyridoxine leeches out of vegetables when they are boiled but can be recovered if the water is used, for example, as soup stock. $1-1\frac{1}{2}$ mg are required daily.

Vitamin B_6 is a mixture of pyridoxine, pyridoxamine and pyridoxal, the three forms differing from each other only very slightly.

Receptor

A molecule in a cell membrane which forms a temporary compound with other molecules leading to a change in the cell's function. No receptor has yet been described in respect of the atoms that make up the molecule, and for this reason receptors remain hypothetical entities. Nevertheless, there are at least four kinds of indirect evidence that they exist:

(1) An estimate can be made of the number of receptors in a cell and of the number of foreign molecules they could bind. Such estimates compare favourably with experimental data.

(2) The nature and time-course of events following the binding of a known molecule to a receptor can be predicted. Again, the estimate is supported experimentally.

(3) The atomic constituents needed to make up the putative receptor can be identified at the site of the receptor-like activity.

(4) No other hypothesis can explain with equal efficiency the activities of *antibodies, antigens, hormones, transmitters* and drugs of all kinds.

The theory of receptors originated with the German bacteriologist, Paul Ehrlich, about 1900. He envisioned claw-like molecules on the cell surface which grab drug molecules out of the surrounding fluid. The cell membrane is still the favoured site for receptors although they may also exist on membranes inside some cells. They are thought to be glycoproteins, compounds composed of a *protein* and a *carbohydrate*, inserted between the *lipid* molecules that form the cell membrane. The protein which may be an *enzyme* is inserted into the membrane proper whereas the carbohydrate forms the external 'claw'. Other models are possible, however.

When a foreign molecule is bound to the carbohydrate portion of the receptor, the chemical configuration of the new compound causes the attached protein to change shape. In its changed form, it is capable of altering the cell's behaviour. Thus, the tertiary structure of an enzyme might be altered so that it would catalyze a new function.

Meanwhile, the shift in protein structure reacts on the attached carbohydrate-foreign molecule compound in such a way that the latter is detached and the carbohydrate returns to its original configuration, followed by the protein. Each of these steps has been demonstrated experimentally, for example, in the activity of the transmitter, *acetylcholine*, when it is released from one nerve cell to conduct a signal to another nerve cell or a muscle.

Releasing factor

One of a group of local *hormones* synthesized or secreted by nerve cells (neurons) in a part of the mid-brain, the hypothalamus, affecting cells in the pituitary gland attached to it. A releasing factor migrates in the *blood* to the attached anterior or forward portion of the pituitary stimulating the secretion of one of six or seven hormones: *adrenocorticotropic hormone* (ACTH), *follicle-stimulating hormone* (FSH), *growth hormone* (GH), *luteinizing hormone* (LH), *prolactin, thyroid-stimulating hormone* (TSH) and possibly *melanocyte-stimulating hormone*. It is assumed that there are either six or seven releasing factors, none having yet been definitely identified for prolactin.

In fact only two have been isolated and clearly described. TSH-releasing factor consists of only three *amino acids*. It may be synthesized and secreted by cells in the brain at some distance from the hypothalamus and transported to that centre in the *cerebrospinal fluid*. LH-releasing factor contains ten amino acids. The same substance probably also acts as FSH-releasing factor. Data reported in 1979 suggests that ACTH-releasing factor may be a modified form of the posterior pituitary hormone, *vasopressin*.

Three release-inhibiting factors produced by cells of the hypothalamus have also been identified in animals: GH-release inhibiting factor (GH-RIF), prolactin release inhibiting factor (P-RIH; H = hormone, another designation for these factors) and melanocyte-release inhibiting factor (M-RIH). They have not yet been positively identified in humans. There is also evidence for the existence of at least two release-inhibiting factors which are produced outside the hypothalamus: *somatostatin* inhibiting secretion of growth hormone and a prolactin-inhibiting factor, probably *dopamine*. Somatostatin may be identical to GH-RIF and is secreted by the D cells of the islets of Langerhans in the pancreas.

In the absence of identified release-inhibiting factors, it seems probable that TSH-releasing factor, LH/FSH-releasing factor and ACTH-releasing factor are shut off by rising *blood* levels of the hormones secreted by the targets for the pituitary hormones. For example, TSH-releasing factor causes secretion of TSH. In turn, TSH stimulates the thyroid gland to release *thyroxine*. A rise in the amount of thyroxine in the blood inhibits secretion of TSH-releasing factor. In the same way, the target hormone (thyroxine in the example) may directly inhibit pituitary secretion of TSH. It is also probable that declining blood levels of the target hormones are a signal for secretion of the appropriate releasing factor. Other signals would originate in the brain itself. Thus, fear causes massive secretion of ACTH-releasing factor.

Releasing factors are delivered to the anterior pituitary in the blood. Although it is part of the general circulation, a localized blood supply flows through the portal system between the hypothalamus and the pituitary, thus limiting the tissues reached by the releasing factors.

Perhaps the most interesting aspect of these chemicals is the physical connection that they make between brain cells and the endocrine system (see *hormone*). They are clear evidence of the physical relationship between brain states and physiological events such as *carbohydrate* utilization and growth.

An important new application of LH-releasing factor was announced late in 1981. The chemical is being tested as a male contraceptive pill. In normal physiological circumstances, it causes the release of interstitial cell-stimulating hormone, the name for male LH, which prepares the testes to produce sperm, but in continuous doses, its effect is the reverse. The sperm count is decisively reduced. This may be another example of the paradoxical effect sometimes seen with the sex hormones (see *oestrogen, progesterone, prolactin, testosterone*).

Renin

An *enzyme* which converts one of the *globulins* in the *blood* to *angiotensin*. Thus, renin is the first step in production of the *hormone, aldosterone*. Renin is synthesized in response to a fall in blood pressure or blood volume. It acts to restore both to their normal values.

Renin takes its name from renal. It is formed by kidney cells also involved in the first step in filtering water, waste and *electrolytes* out of the blood. It should not be confused with rennin which clots the milk protein, casein, and is found in the stomachs of young mammals including human infants.

In the kidney, the first filtration is accomplished by a tiny sack called a glomerulus. There are millions of glomeruli in or near the kidney cortex in close association with capillaries. They are capable of removing all liquid from the body in about two minutes! Obviously, a very high proportion of water – some 99 per cent – must be reabsorbed into the blood. The machinery of reabsorption is the long tubules which link each glomerulus to the urinary tract at the centre of the kidney. The exact amount of water reabsorbed depends on the *acid–base* state of *body fluids* and the relative density of other blood constituents. Blood volume and therefore blood pressure are kept in balance with the body fluids by the osmotic pressure between them. Osmotic pressure is in turn determined by the *proteins*, electrolytes and other constituents of the two compartments. The kidneys play their role by reabsorbing not only water but electrolytes from the glomerular filtrate. The renin-angiotensin-aldosterone system is part of the regulatory process.

Reverse transcriptase (see *Ribonucleic acid*)

Rhodopsin (see *Iodopsin*)

Riboflavin (*Vitamin* B_2)

A vitamin-B_2 deficiency causes no distinctive disease like beri-beri (see *thiamine*), but the symptoms of deficiency include rough, scaly skin, swelling and cracking of the lips and degeneration of the cornea of the eye. Many other diseases cause similar disorders, however, and correct diagnosis of riboflavin deficiency often depends on the appearance of symptoms more clearly connected to other vitamin deficiencies. If the diet lacks riboflavin, it may also lack the other B vitamins.

The richest sources are liver, kidney, eggs and milk. Dark green vegetables such as broccoli tops are also good, but boiling leeches riboflavin as it does the other B vitamins. It can be recovered if the water is used, for example, as soup stock. The basic requirement is about one to two milligrams per day for adults, easily supplied by the average western diet. Children and pregnant women need somewhat larger amounts. It is not possible to take too much riboflavin because like all B vitamins it is water soluble and is excreted in the urine.

Riboflavin is needed to synthesize a *coenzyme*, flavin adenine dinucleotide (FAD). Like the chemically-similar coenzyme, *nicotinamide adenine dinucleotide*, FAD plays its role in association with enzymes catalyzing the creation and storage of energy. The structural formula of riboflavin is:

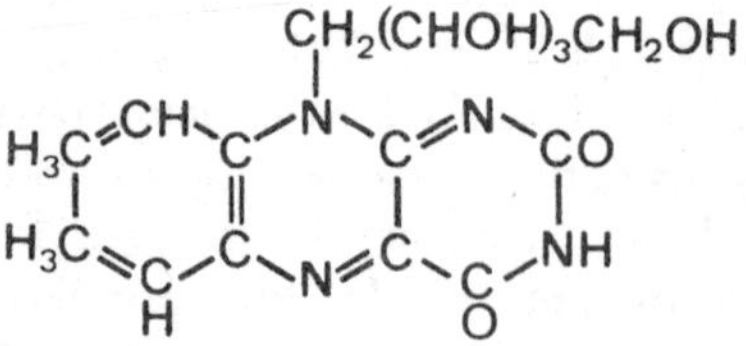

Ribonucleic acid (RNA)

The chemical transcribed from the genetic molecule, *deoxyribonucleic acid* (DNA), which can be translated into *protein*. RNA is the intermediate step in the conversion of genotype to phenotype; that is, the process of converting genes to physical characteristics.

In fact, there are at least three kinds of RNA: messenger RNA (mRNA) consists of a long chain of *nucleotides* complementary to the DNA nucleotides forming a gene. Thus, each mRNA molecule is the transcription of a gene. It is formed in the cell nucleus and migrates to the cytoplasm where it becomes attached to a cellular organelle called a ribosome.

The ribosome is a protein-making machine. It has a larger and a smaller segment, both of which are made principally of the second kind of RNA, ribosomal RNA (rRNA), plus protein and some other chemicals. Ribosomal RNA is presumably also transcribed from genes in the nucleus, but the evidence is far from conclusive. It is at least possible that rRNA is synthesized on a template provided by existing rRNA without DNA. In any case, mRNA becomes attached to the larger segment of a ribosome and is moved through the machine like a ratchet bar by the action of the smaller segment. As the mRNA is moved through the ribosome, each codon or 3-*base* genetic code word picks up the correct *amino acid* which is connected by a *peptide* bond to the amino acid immediately preceding it.

The amino acids are fetched out of the cytoplasm by the third kind of RNA, transfer RNA (tRNA). Each tRNA molecule is also presumably formed on a DNA template in the nucleus, but because of their base sequences, these nucleic acids take up complex cloverleaf formations. One end of the cloverleaf also contains a codon for an amino acid. Another sequence of bases causes the tRNA to attach itself temporarily to the ribosome where it makes the amino acid available to the mRNA. Many of the physical relationships necessary for these machine-tool like operations have been worked out theoretically using basic knowledge of the tiny electrical forces exerted by atoms alone and in compounds, but the events themselves involve structures too small to be seen in action with existing technology.

RNA differs from DNA in two respects: (1) the ribose sugar in each nucleotide contains one more *oxygen* atom than the ribose in the DNA nucleotide, (2) the base, *thymine*, is replaced in RNA by the base, *uracil*. Uracil and thymine are of the same chemical family, the pyrimidines, and the substitution in RNA is required chemically because of the difference in the sugar.

The Watson–Crick model of DNA and its function in the transmission of genetic information also implied if it did not state absolutely that the biosynthetic sequence of DNA→RNA→protein is invariable. There is now overwhelming evidence that the sequence is DNA⇆RNA→protein. The discovery of the *enzyme*, reverse transcriptase, is perhaps the most conclusive evidence that under certain conditions DNA is synthesized from an RNA template because the enzyme catalyzes the process. At present, this correct sequence is of potential significance in the understanding of cancer. Several viruses have been implicated as causes of cancer, but in some of them, the genetic material is RNA. It had been supposed that a virus might help to cause cancer when its nucleic acid became a part of the cell's nucleic acid. An analogous process involving a free sequence of nucleotides rather than a virus underlies the manipulation known as genetic engineering. The viral theory of cancer causation received considerable support, therefore, from the discovery of reverse transcriptase.

The enzyme also introduces another controversial possibility. The original Watson–Crick model confirmed the Darwinian theory of inheritance which displaced the older Lamarckian theory based on inheritance of acquired characteristics. That is, the genes alone act as templates for phenotypic expression. It was not possible that acquired phenotypes could alter the DNA composing the genes. Reverse transcriptase opens the way to a reinstatement of the Lamarckian notion that acquired characteristics can be inherited because it provides a mechanism whereby at least one acquired characteristic – a viral infection – could alter the genetic material and be passed through the parents' germ cells to their children.

Ribose

A simple sugar found in the nucleic acids, *deoxyribonucleic acid* and *ribonucleic acid* and in *nucleotides* such as *nicotinamide adenine dinucleotide.*

Ribose is synthesized by most cells and found in all natural foods. In organic compounds, it is a pentose sugar with a five-membered ring:

In the free state, the molecule may take up a six-member-ring conformation.

Saliva

A watery secretion in the mouth from glands in the cheeks and beneath the jaws which helps to lubricate food for swallowing, enhances the sense of taste, begins digestion, facilitates speech and helps to keep the mouth and teeth clean.

Saliva is secreted by three pairs of exocrine glands; that is, glands using ducts to carry their secretions to the site of action. The parotid glands in the cheeks secrete about 25 per cent of the saliva. About 70 per cent comes from the submandibular glands beneath the jaw under the back teeth, and the remaining 5 per cent is secreted by the sublingual glands in the forward part of the mouth floor. About 500 ml are secreted per day. The glands respond to reflex stimulation originating either in the taste buds or in brain centres such as the cortex; for example, to thoughts of food. Signals to the glands are conveyed by parasympathetic nerves of the involuntary nervous system (see *transmitter*). Excitement or fear can inhibit salivation. The approach of vomiting causes salivation as part of a widespread activation of the involuntary nervous system.

Only about 0.5 per cent of saliva is solid matter, and most of this is *protein*. Mucin, a glycoprotein or protein to which a *carbohydrate* is attached, gives the fluid viscosity and increases its value as a lubricant. The water dissolves food constituents which then stimulate the taste buds, specialized nerve endings that respond to sweet, sour, salt or bitter. Saliva also contains ptyalin, probably the same *enzyme* as pancreatic *amylase* which breaks down starch to *maltose*. However, food stays in the mouth too short a time for ptyalin to have much effect, and the enzyme is rapidly destroyed by gastric acids (see *hydrochloric acid, pepsin*). Ptyalin may also act as a bactericide, killing germs in the mouth. Other *lysozymes* are present which further clean the mouth and teeth. Saliva also washes the buccal cavity. It contains buffers, especially bicarbonate (see *carbonic acid*). They normally assure a neutral or slightly alkaline pH (see Appendix 2). If it is too acid, saliva may dissolve *calcium* in tooth *enamel* forming a complex substance called calculus. Speech is facilitated because of the lubricating action of saliva in the mouth and on the tongue and teeth.

Mumps is the only common disease affecting the salivary glands.

Salt

(1) Sodium chloride, NaCl, ordinary table salt. (2) A chemical compound formed by neutralizing an *acid* with a *base*, usually with the additional formation of water.

The chemical nature of the base in definition (2) is not so easily specified. In chemistry, a salt is defined as a compound formed by reaction between an acid and a mineral. Thus, *hydrochloric acid* combines with *sodium* to form sodium chloride. In biochemistry, a great many salts are formed in exactly the same way; that is, by combination of a mineral and an acid. Organic acids may also form salts with ammonia, NH_3, as well as by losing *hydrogen*; in other words, by oxidation (see *cytochrome*). Thus, lactic acid is converted to lactate, a salt, by oxidation in muscle cells and provides a small energy increment during heavy exercise (see *lactose*). In other words, the common denominator of all salts, organic and inorganic, is the loss of hydrogen by an acid whether or not the hydrogen is replaced by another atom or atomic group.

Sodium chloride is present in all *body fluids* and provides the principal source of both sodium and chloride *ions* which are required for many physiological functions such as the electrochemical signals of nerve cells. The importance of salt is said to reflect the origin of life in sea water.

The proper balance of salt and water is the function of the kidneys. Vomiting, fluid leakage through severe burns, and in hot weather excessive sweating, lower the salt content of the body. The effect is to lower salt concentrations in body fluids. Muscular weakness and cramp commonly follow and may lead to tetanic seizures. Conversely, if *blood* circulation is poor because of heart or blood vessel diseases or if the kidneys malfunction, too much salt is retained. Water is then also retained to maintain a proper balance. The result is a swelling called oedema. The kidneys can allow a concentration of salt in urine up to 2 per cent, but they cannot increase the amount excreted beyond that figure. That is why sea water is a poison: its salt content is about 3 per cent. To eliminate the salt from a pint of sea water, the kidneys must excrete 1½ pints of water. The only source for the extra half pint is the body fluid so that rapid and fatal dehydration ensues.

Patients with heart or blood vessel disease are often placed on a low salt diet. A salt substitute like potassium chloride (the *potassium* salt of hydrochloric acid) may be used for seasoning. Most of us, however, must replace the small salt losses from sweating, about a gram a day. Our average daily intake is far in excess of this, about 10 to 15 grams.

Semen (L.: *seminis* (gen) = of seed)

A thick, whitish fluid secreted by male reproductive organs. It consists of sperm in their plasma and secretions from the seminal vesicles, the prostate and other glands connected to the urethra, the tube which also conducts urine from the bladder through the penis. Semen acts as a nutrient vehicle for sperm and contains *enzymes* required to enable the sperm to penetrate and fertilize the ovum. Conditions in the vaginal *mucus* and the uterus itself are also relevant to the success of fertilization, however.

Semen originates with spermatogenesis, sperm formation, in the seminiferous tubules of the testes. The process is probably regulated by *follicle-stimulating hormone* (FSH) and interstitial cell-stimulating hormone (see *luteinizing hormone*) secreted by the pituitary gland. The sperm become motile only after they have left the seminiferous tubules and entered the epididymus, still within the testes. Motility is associated with viability because the sperm must make their own way into the uterus from the upper vaginal tract. However, in the process of ejaculation, the sperm must pass first up the vas deferens or seminal tract to the prostate even before they leave the urethra.

Just before the prostate, seminal vesicles add an amount of fluid equalling about 60 per cent of the final volume. Seminal fluid is yellowish from the *flavoproteins* it contains, and slightly alkaline despite some *ascorbic acid* (*vitamin* C). Seminal fluid also contains *prostaglandins* which may be partly responsible for the force of ejaculation. *Fructose* in the seminal fluid is thought to act as a nutrient for the sperm.

The prostate adds about 20 per cent of final volume. This portion is slightly *acid* because it contains *citric acid* and some enzymes. The final pH of semen is about 7.4, or slightly alkaline (see Appendix 2). Any significant variation destroys the sperm.

About three millilitres of semen containing some 200 million sperms is released with each ejaculation. If the sperm count falls below 20 million per ml, the man is probably infertile. Such are the odds against fertilization despite the fact that only one sperm is required to fertilize the single egg normally available in the human uterus each month.

Semen is continuously produced, especially in younger men. If ejaculation does not take place, erections and discharge at night – wet dreams – are common. They are physiological events that occur independently of mental attitudes.

Serotonin (5-Hydroxytryptamine, 5-HT)

A local *hormone* which plays a role in *blood* clotting, and a *transmitter* of signals between nerve cells or neurons in some parts of the brain.

Serotonin is released by platelets and causes constriction of muscle cells in small blood vessels, thus assisting the clotting process. It is also secreted by cells lining the intestinal wall, and it may be that 5-HT in blood is in part at least produced by gut cells.

As a transmitter, serotonin may both excite and inhibit neurons, depending on the part of the brain where it appears. In the pineal body near the centre of the brain, for example, it is inhibitory. In brain centres that regulate emotions, it is excitatory.

Anti-depressant drugs, including the *monoamine oxidase* inhibitors, increase the amount of 5-HT in the brain. Hallucinogenic drugs such as LSD (lysergic acid diethylamide) mimic and exaggerate the effects of serotonin. The LSD molecule contains within it a segment which resembles the serotonin molecule.

It is an *amino acid* which is synthesized by nerve cells and other cells from another amino acid, tryptophan. Its structural formula is:

$$HO-\text{(ring)}-CH_2-CH_2-NH_2$$

Sodium (Na) (L.: *natrium*)

A soft, silvery metallic element found in all *body fluids* and in cells. Sodium is the chief cation or positive *ion* in the body other than *hydrogen*. In cells, it may be replaced by *potassium*. Sodium is needed for correct *bone* structure, to permit nerve and muscle cells to function, and to maintain the *acid–base* balance of the body.

Most dietary sodium is taken as *salt*, sodium chloride. Some is also obtained indirectly from foods containing it such as meat, fish, eggs and milk. A salt-free diet which includes these foods will supply about half a gram of sodium per day.

The average adult body contains 75 to 100 grams about 90 per cent of which is dissolved in the body fluids. The kidneys regulate sodium excretion, shutting down urinary loss of the ion if necessary, but some sodium is excreted in sweat. In tropical weather, the sweat loss alone must be made good.

Among the most prominent symptoms of severe sodium deficiency are muscular cramp, convulsions and eventually, coma. These signs reflect the loss of excitability by nerve and muscle cells, the cause of which can best be explained by describing the normal nerve signal. (See also *potassium*). The nerve cell or neuron consists of three parts: dendrites, the heavily arborized processes that receive signals from other neurons; the cell body containing the cell's biosynthetic machinery and genetic material, also capable of receiving signals from other neurons; and the axon. The axon extends from the cell body as a single process or it may have infrequent branches. It maintains its thickness throughout, having tiny swellings or axon bulbs at the tip of each branch. Although the axons of brain neurons may be no more than a few millimetres in length, those in the legs of adults extend for a metre or more from the foot to the spinal cord. The axon conducts the nerve signal away from the cell body to the next neuron.

The entire neuron is enclosed by a membrane, like all cells, but the neuronal membrane maintains the interior of the cell in an electrically-negative state with respect to the surrounding body fluid. The principal ion in the axon is *chlorine* (Cl^-), but there is also some potassium, a positive ion. When the neuron is about to signal, the axon membrane where it emerges from the cell body suddenly allows sodium in the body fluid to enter the cell flowing down the gradient from high concentration to low. This inward flow may also be assisted by an *enzyme* in the cell membrane. Within two or three milliseconds, the influx of sodium ions has changed the cell's charge from negative to positive. Meanwhile, some potassium has begun to leave the cell, but this loss of positive ions is not at first enough to prevent the rapid build up of a positive charge inside the cell. Within about six milliseconds of the first inward surge, the membrane has again changed its state and an enzyme is actively pumping sodium out of the axon. Within 10 milliseconds, therefore, the negative interior charge is restored. *Calcium* ions both inside and outside the cell are also essential to this process.

The sodium that has entered the cell has initiated a change in the membrane state proximal to the initial point of entry, thus moving the signal along the axon. Because the signal represents a reversal of the cell's potential in the electrical sense, the signal is known as an action potential.

The events leading to the contraction of *myosin* along the actin molecule in muscle cells are analogous to those in neurons in respect to the role played by sodium. In the absence of sodium, therefore, excitable cells malfunction.

Sodium has atomic number 11 and atomic weight 22.990.

Somatostatin

A *hormone* secreted by cells in the islets of Langerhans in the pancreas and possibly by brain cells in the mid-brain region, the hypothalamus. Somatostatin acts in the hypothalamus as an inhibitor of *growth hormone releasing factor*, thus halting the secretion of growth hormone by the pituitary gland. Indeed, it may be the same as growth hormone-release inhibiting factor which is secreted by the hypothalamus in some animals. Somatostatin may also inhibit the secretion of *aldosterone* by the adrenal cortex.

It is a *peptide* containing 14 *amino acids* secreted by D cells in the islets. *Glucagon* is secreted by A cells and *insulin*, by B cells. Somatostatin acts in concert with these hormones to regulate the use of *glucose* in body cells and its availability in the *blood*. If the effect on aldosterone output is confirmed, somatostatin may also regulate the *mineral* content of *body fluids*. The relationships between these roles and the inhibition of growth hormone secretion is not clear.

Somatotrophin (see *Growth hormone*)

Steapsin (see *Lipase*)

Steroid

One of a class of compounds consisting of a 17-carbon, four-ring (see Appendix 1) structure called the perhydrocyclopentenophenanthrene (per-hydro-cyclo-penteno-phenan-threne) ring, thus:

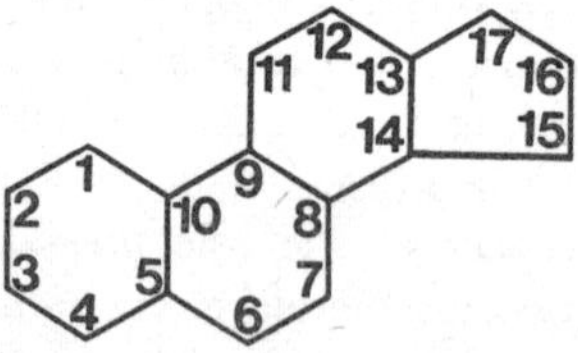

Steroids include the *bile salts, cholesterol,* the *adrenocorticosteroid hormones* and the molecule from which *vitamin* D is synthesized by the action of sunlight on the skin. Steroids are part of the larger class of *lipids.*

The numbers in the structural diagram are the accepted enumeration of the *carbon* atoms. Functional differences amongst the steroids arise from the different atoms attached to the various carbon atoms. For an example, see the structural diagram of *cholesterol.* Oestradiol, the most active form of the female hormone, *oestrogen,* has two hydroxyl (OH) groups at carbon 3 and 17, respectively, a hydrogen at carbon 13 and double bonds between carbons 1 and 2, 3 and 4 and 5 and 10.

Substance P (see *Transmitter*)

Sugar

(1) Sucrose, ordinary table sugar, (2) a sweet *carbohydrate* of animal or vegetable origin, (3) *blood* sugar; that is, the *glucose* content of the blood.

All sugars consist of molecules with the general formula, $C_nH_{2n}O_n$, in which n = the number of atoms. Sugars are either monosaccharides (L.: *saccharum*; Gr.: *sakcharon* = sugar), disaccharides or polysaccharides depending on whether they consist of one molecule with the general formula, two molecules or three or more, respectively. Sucrose is a disaccharide consisting of glucose plus *fructose*, both monosaccharides. Sucrose and fructose are found only in vegetables whereas glucose is common to animals and vegetables. *Maltose* is also a disaccharide made up of two molecules of glucose. *Lactose* is glucose plus *galactose*. *Glycogen*, a long chain of glucose molecules, is a polysaccharide.

Many sugar molecules assume different forms depending on the relationship of the atoms within the general formula. Form does not appear to affect their chemical characteristics or their sweetness. For example, glucose and fructose may exist in either a six-ring form:

or a five-ring form:

named the pyranose and furanose forms, respectively. In the body, all of the sugars named except lactose are converted to glucose and broken down to supply energy (see *citric acid*).

It is for this reason that blood sugar is an important sign of health or disease. If the blood sugar is elevated above normal as in diabetes, the cells may be starved because the glucose is not being taken up. Abnormally low blood sugar is less common but no less serious a disorder. It may occur in a diabetic who has had too high an insulin dose, but low blood sugar can occur in non-diabetics after stress, and after large doses of aspirin and some antihistamines (see *histamine*).

Excess sugar is excreted in the urine. Indeed, one test for diabetes used to be tasting the patient's urine.

Sulphur (US: Sulfur; S)

A non-metallic element present in two *amino acids*, cysteine and methionine, and therefore, part of many proteins. Atoms of sulphur form cross-links between amino acids containing them. The links may connect two amino acids in the same chain, as in *oxytocin* and *vasopressin*, or the links may join two chains, as in *antibodies* and *insulin*. When the link connects two molecules of cysteine, the combined molecule may be called cystine.

Thiamine and another B *vitamin*, biotin, also contain sulphur. Methionine, like the vitamins, is an essential nutrient, but because sulphur is available in most food, there is no other special dietary requirement. Sulphur is excreted as sulphate in the urine at the rate of about a gram per day.

Sulphur is a yellowish-orange powder or gas. Its atomic number is 16 and atomic weight, 32.064.

Sweat

A watery fluid secreted by sweat glands for the purpose of cooling the skin by evaporation. Evaporation is accomplished by means of heat from within the body, not by the environmental heat. Body heat can be elevated because of environmental heat, however, as well as by exercise or fever.

Sweating is an active process requiring selective removal of substances from the *blood* and other *body fluids*. Water is also lost through the skin as perspiration, a passive event properly called imperceptible or insensible perspiration. The skin is not a water-tight sheath, and in temperate climates, water loss due to seepage and evaporation amounts to 900 ml or nearly a litre a day. This will probably rise in hot weather and fall in cold. Like sweat, perspiration in humid conditions cannot cool the body because evaporation does not take place.

Sweat is primarily water. It contains *salt* (*sodium* chloride), but at a concentration lower than that in the blood. Normally the other contents of sweat are small amounts of *potassium*, lactate (see *lactose*) from the operation of the sweat glands themselves, and kallikrin, the *enzyme* which catalyzes the biosynthesis of *bradykinin*. The role of bradykinin is to stimulate the enlargement of blood vessels in the skin increasing the blood flow and heat loss.

There are two types of sweat gland: eccrine and apocrine. Eccrine glands are under the control of the sympathetic division of the involuntary nervous system (see *transmitter*). The amount of salt in the sweat they secrete is regulated in part by the *hormone, aldosterone*. They are widely distributed in the skin.

Apocrine glands are found in the armpits, nipples and vulva. They are not under nervous control but are stimulated by *adrenaline* in the blood. Apocrine sweat is milky and odourless until it is subjected to the activity of skin-surface bacteria which cause it to develop a characteristic smell.

Aluminium- and zinc-containing compounds inhibit apocrine sweating and the growth of skin-bacteria. They are used in all body deodorants.

On a hot, dry day, the body can lose up to 4 litres of water. Obviously, it must be replaced fairly continuously. If it is not, dehydration causes body temperature to rise sharply. The salt loss must also be made up if heat stroke is to be avoided.

About half the sweat comes from the skin of the trunk, a quarter from the lower limbs and the balance from the head and upper limbs. It is possible to distinguish two kinds of sweating, probably related to the two types of sweat glands: in the heat, sweat appears almost simultaneously on all skin areas but most noticeably on the forehead, upper lip, neck and chest. Mental or emotional stimuli, on the other hand, cause sweating which is largely confined to the palms, soles and armpits.

Sweat gland secretion can be monitored by measuring the electrical resistance of the skin. Resistance declines as sweating increases because of the increased amount of water. This physical event underlies lie detectors as well as physiological tests to establish the intensity of emotional states.

Modified sweat glands in the outer ear, the ceruminous glands, secrete ear wax.

Synovial fluid

(Synovia) (Gr.: *syn* = with + *öon* = egg)

A viscid, transparent fluid secreted by cells in the membranes lining joints and tendon sheaths. It has the appearance of egg white, and therefore its name.

Synovial fluid is a lubricant for joints. It is held within the joint by the synovial membrane. Its physical properties derive from small amounts of *hyaluronic acid* linked to a *protein*. When the limb is quiet or moving slowly, these large molecules are thought to be coiled in a helical form. With rapid movement, they may uncoil to reduce friction by reducing the fluid thickness, like oil thinning as it heats up in a car engine.

Tears

The slightly *salt* secretion of the lachrymal glands in the orbits of the eyeballs. They serve as a lubricant and bactericide.

The liquid is mostly water and because of the filtering action of the cells in the lachrymal glands, it contains less salt than the *blood*. Tears are discharged through ducts into the upper conjunctiva, the linings of the eyelids. On the corneas, tears form a film which is renewed by blinking. Secretion normally keeps pace with drying of the conjunctiva and is thus responsive to environmental temperature and humidity. If foreign bodies or irritants enter the eye, more tears are secreted to dilute the invasive substance. Of course, lachrymal secretion is also under nervous control and responds to emotional stress. Because secretion is normally related to need, one is usually unaware of tears, but an excess falls over the lower eyelid and some is drained away by ducts in the lower lid leading indirectly into the nose.

Tears contain bicarbonate (see *carbonic acid*) and are slightly alkaline (pH: 7.4; see Appendix 2). The bactericidal agent is the *enzyme, lysozyme*. Note that both natural substances and drugs may be bacteriostatic, in which case they tend to stop bacterial multiplication, or they may kill bacteria. The latter are bactericides. Lysozyme kills bacteria in the conjunctiva.

Testosterone

The male sex *hormone* secreted by the testes.

The testes perform two roles: they produce sperm (see *semen*), and they also act as an endocrine gland secreting testosterone. The hormone is synthesized by interstitial cells under the influence of interstitial cell-stimulating hormone (ICSH; see *luteinizing hormone*) from the pituitary gland. ICSH in turn is thought to be secreted in response to a *releasing factor* produced by nerve cells in the hypothalamus, the mid-brain centre to which the pituitary is attached. Testosterone in the *blood* does not appear to cut off secretion of a releasing factor; thus, it is not part of a feedback mechanism like that which regulates the female hormones. On the other hand, blood levels of testosterone may affect the pituitary secretion of ICSH directly, a 'short loop' feedback.

Testosterone secretion begins at puberty causing development of male secondary sexual characteristics: hair distribution, enlargement of the genitals, and enlargement of the larynx leading to deepening of the voice. The hormone also stimulates growth by increasing the utilization of *amino acids* and *proteins*. Part of its action is analogous to that of *growth hormone*. Used as a drug to correct dwarfism due to pituitary deficiency of growth hormone, testosterone aids growth and maturation. Yet excessive doses may actually inhibit the growth of long *bones*.

Testosterone or related chemicals may also help to correct impotence due to malformed testicles. In most cases of impotence, however, the disorder is psychological, reflecting unsatisfactory sexual activity rather than glandular deficiency. Impotent men often find that their problem disappears with a new sex partner.

Testosterone or related chemicals may help to control breast cancer. The probable explanation for this use is that

175

the male hormone antagonizes the female hormone, *oestrogen*, which seems to exacerbate the cancer under some circumstances. Used as a drug for women, testosterone causes virilization.

In searching for a male contraceptive pill, attempts have been made to develop *androgens*, the generic term for male hormones, that inhibit or antagonize testosterone; that is, anti-androgens. The effect must of course be reversible. Although several such chemicals exist, they have not yet been successful, in part perhaps because of the psychological difficulty men experience in voluntarily inducing infertility. Nevertheless, research continues, and in the early 1980s explored the value of *luteinizing hormone releasing factor*, neither an androgen nor specifically an anti-androgen, as a male pill (see *releasing factor*). Incidentally, the androgens used by athletes illegally to build up muscle are in most instances chemically-related to testosterone, and any of them may produce temporary impotence.

Testosterone is a *steroid*. It is the most active of several closely related compounds formed in the process of testosterone synthesis from *cholesterol*. It causes increased synthesis of the nucleic acids, *deoxyribonucleic acid* and *ribonucleic acid*, and of protein. The new proteins include *enzymes* that speed up the energy-storage processes in target cells (see *citric acid, cytochrome*), but the relation between these molecular events and the physiological effects of testosterone is not clear.

Thiamine

Vitamin B$_1$, the anti-beriberi factor, identified in 1911 by the German chemist, Funk, and therefore the first vitamin to be isolated. Beriberi is characterized by muscular weakness, disturbance of the senses, heart disorders and oedema or an abnormal increase in tissue fluid resulting in this instance from poor circulation.

The daily requirement of thiamine is very small, between 1.1 and 1.4 mg for men and 0.9 and 1 mg for women. The average diet contains much more. Yeast, cereal germ and bran, peanuts and cod are probably the richest sources. As with other B vitamins, boiling leeches thiamine out of vegetables, but it can be recovered if the water is used, for example as soup stock. Toasting bread for a minute removes about a third of the vitamin in the slice. Roughly the same amount is lost when meat is cooked. Freezing does not diminish thiamine content, but it is reduced up to 40 per cent over six months by frozen storage. Nevertheless, the only westerners normally at risk from thiamine deficiency are heavy drinkers who eat too little.

Thiamine is required to synthesize the *coenzyme*, thiamine pyrophosphate, which participates in the oxidation (see *cytochrome*) of pyruvic acid at the beginning of the citric acid cycle. Thus, like *niacin* and *riboflavin*, thiamine contributes to the process by which *glucose* is broken down to obtain energy.

Thrombin (see *Blood factor*)

Thymine

A *base* found in some *nucleotides* and in *deoxyribonucleic acid* (DNA). In *ribonucleic acid*, thymine is replaced by another base, *uracil*. The complementary base to thymine in the DNA double helix is *adenine*.

Thymine is one of a class of compounds called pyrimidines. Its structural formula is:

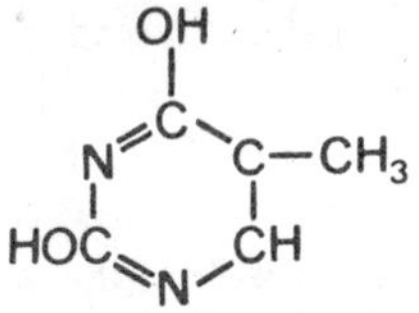

Thyroid stimulating hormone (TSH; Thyrotropin)

A *hormone* secreted by the anterior or forward part of the pituitary gland which stimulates the thyroid gland to produce *thyroxine*. The secretion of TSH is regulated both by

177

the direct feedback to the pituitary of thyroxine in the *blood* and by a second hormone, TSH-*releasing factor*. The releasing factor is probably secreted by nerve cells in the hypothalamus, a segment of the mid-brain above the pituitary to which the gland is attached. TSH-releasing factor secretion is also responsive to the amount of thyroxine in the blood and to environmental factors. Nerve cells in the hypothalamus respond to temperature changes, and cold causes the secretion of TSH-releasing factor.

In cells of the thyroid glands, TSH activates *cyclic adenosine monophosphate* (cAMP), the so-called second messenger, causing the cells to take up more oxygen and glucose from the blood. Oxygen and glucose are the sources of additional energy. Cyclic-AMP also activates *enzymes* which split thyroxine off from the *protein* to which it has been bound for storage.

TSH is a glycoprotein; that is, a protein with a *carbohydrate* bound to it. The hormone has been purified for clinical use to distinguish thyroid insufficiency (really, thyroxine insufficiency) due to pituitary failure from other types. If the thyroxine output rises in response to TSH, there has been pituitary failure, but if there is no increase in thyroxine output, the problem lies elsewhere, probably in the thyroid gland itself.

Thyroxine

A *hormone* secreted by the thyroid gland which helps to regulate the speed and amount of chemical activity – that is, the metabolism – of body cells. The thyroid is an endocrine gland (described under *hormone*) lying at the base of the neck with a lobe on either side of the windpipe joined across the front by an isthmus of thyroid tissue so that it looks like a butterfly. Calcitonin is also a thyroid hormone, but it plays a role in *calcium* use.

Thyroxine causes an increase in chemical activity, raising *oxygen* consumption and the breakdown of *glucose*, but much of the energy produced is lost as heat rather than being stored. Nevertheless, thyroxine promotes growth and development of the tissues, perhaps because cellular biosynthetic processes and cell division are speeded up.

Hormone output begins in foetal life, reaches a peak during middle life and declines with age. The normal *blood* level of thyroxine in middle life maintains metabolism at a rate which produces 40 Cal per square metre in men and 37 Cal in women. A gram of thyroxine given by mouth increases the average daily caloric intake required from 2500 to 3500. Thus, if the patient given thyroxine maintains a diet of 2500 Cal, he will lose weight. Increasing the amount of thyroxine in the *blood* also reduces the blood concentration of *cholesterol* despite an increase in synthetic activity by the liver. By burning up calorific chemicals, the thyroid hormone is useful both in the treatment of obesity and as a means of reducing the danger of arterial blockage. Such blockages can cause a heart attack, and they are related statistically to blood cholesterol level. Unfortunately, thyroxine also causes a speed up in heart muscle action which can lead to erratic heart beat or even heart failure.

Underactivity of the thyroid causes a fall in metabolism to as little as 50 per cent of normal. Body temperature remains below 37 degrees C, heart rate and blood pressure decline and blood cholesterol level rises. The condition may be caused by disease, but it can also be inherited. Infants who suffer from thyroid deficiency may become cretins. Thyroxine can prevent this if the need for it is recognized in time to avoid permanent damage to the brain and body, but unfortunately, this is seldom the case. In adults, thyroid insufficiency causes myxoedema (Gr.: *myx* = muscle + *oedema* = swelling), so called because fluid accumulates in the tissues causing weight gain and swelling. Thyroxine effectively treats myxoedema. Thyroid deficiency may also be caused by a lack of *iodine* in the diet, but the practice of adding it to all *salt* is now widespread.

Overactivity of the thyroid, hyperthyroidism, can be due to any one of three causes: a disorder in the gland itself, an excess of *thyroid-stimulating hormone* (TSH) from the pituitary gland, or a compound called long-acting thyroid stimulator found in the blood plasma of some hyperthyroid patients.

Overactivity causes an increase in metabolism with a rise in oxygen consumption, heat production and heart rate. The patient usually feels too warm and is nervous and irritable. Iodine can help hyperthyroidism for a short time, but surgical removal of as much as three-quarters of the thyroid gland may be the only successful treatment.

Goitre, the swelling of the thyroid, used to be a fairly common sight at any distance from the sea because of the absence of iodine from the soil. In fact, the swelling can reflect thyroid overactivity as well as the reverse. Thus, although the goitre of iodine shortage reflects an enlargement of the gland to overcome the deficiency, it may be caused by the presence of too much TSH which also causes the gland to swell. In other words, goitre indicates that something is wrong with the thyroid, but the discovery of the ultimate cause may require sophisticated laboratory analysis.

The cellular mechanism of action of thyroxine is not fully understood. Like some other hormones, it stimulates *ribonucleic acid* synthesis and thereby probably increases the quantity and activity of *enzymes* in the cell's power house, the organelles called mitochondria, where glucose is broken down in the *citric acid* cycle and the energy thus obtained is stored by oxidative phosphorylation (see *cytochrome*). These events would explain the increased need for glucose and oxygen in the presence of thyroxine, but the synthesis of the energy-storage molecule, *adenosine triphosphate*, is less than would be expected.

Thyroxine is a small molecule synthesized from the *amino acid*, tyrosine. Thyroid cells add iodine obtained from iodide in salt and many food substances. Thyroxine consists of tyrosine plus four iodine atoms. A modified form of the hormone, triiodothyroxine, has only three atoms of iodine. In the structural formula, the I in the dotted circle is missing in triiodothyroxine:

In other endocrine glands, hormones are secreted into the blood as soon as they are synthesized. In the thyroid, secretory cells line vesicles filled with a storage medium, a *protein* to which thyroxine is bound until it is needed. An enzyme in the thyroid then splits the thyroxine from the protein, but it is carried in the blood mainly in combination with another protein, alpha-*globulin*.

Thyroxine regulates its own secretion by a feedback arrangement affecting both the mid-brain region, the hypothalamus, and the pituitary gland below it. A fall in blood level of thyroxine causes hypothalamic nerve cells to secrete thyroid-stimulating hormone *releasing factor* (TSH-RF). TSH-RF is transmitted in the local blood supply to the pituitary where cells in the anterior or forward part of the gland secrete TSH into the blood. TSH causes thyroxine to split off from its storage protein so that it is secreted into the blood, and the rise in blood thyroxine shuts off TSH-RF.

Tranquillizer, natural

This entry should be read in conjunction with *endorphin*.

A natural body chemical which acts in the brain to control anxiety and depression, and which may induce sleep.

The chemical has been isolated from the brains of experimental animals, but it has not yet been analysed. It appears to be a small molecule like the endorphins, and it is thought to inhibit the activity of some nerve cells or neurons, particularly in the mid-brain region that regulates the emotions.

The natural tranquillizer was isolated during the last years of the 1970s because research workers followed the same line of reasoning that had been applied to the discovery of the natural opiates, the endorphins and enkephalins. Tranquillizers reduce the sense of tension and fear by binding to *receptors* in neurons and altering their behaviour. Such receptors must have evolved along with a naturally occurring tranquillizer. Whether the substance discovered in laboratory animals exists in man remains to be seen, but again by analogy with the natural opiates, it seems likely.

Transmitter

A chemical released as a result of the signal in a nerve cell (neuron) which diffuses across the narrow space (synaptic gap) separating it from the next (post-synaptic) neuron and changes the electrochemical properties of the post-synaptic neuron. For a description of the nerve signal itself, see *sodium*.

The transmitter may either decrease resistance of the neuron cell membrane to the flow of *ions* through it, thus enhancing the readiness of the neuron to signal, or it may increase membrane resistance, decreasing the possibility of a signal. The former is called an excitatory transmitter, and the latter, an inhibitory transmitter. Every neuron may be affected by both excitatory and inhibitory transmitters from other neurons which nearly touch or synapse with it. It has been believed that each neuron synthesizes only one transmitter, but newer evidence places that hypothesis in doubt.

In the brain and at other places in the body where groups of neurons interact (that is, a ganglion; pl.: ganglia), nerve cells add and subtract excitatory and inhibitory signals to reach a signalling threshold themselves. In some cases, moreover, the transmitter may alter the behaviour of the neuron which has released it, causing this pre-synaptic neuron itself to become more or less ready to signal. Thus, each neuron is a tiny calculating machine as well as a signalling device.

A number of transmitters have been identified: see *acetylcholine, dopamine, gamma-amino butyric acid* (GABA), *glutamic acid, glycine, noradrenaline, serotonin*, and also *endorphin* and *tranquillizer, natural*. Several other *amino acids, vasopressin* and a chemical identified only as substance P may also be transmitters. Although no *receptor* has yet been described in detail, there is a growing body of experimental data about the number and location of receptors on neurons and on muscle cells which also respond to transmitters. Artificial manipulation of the transmitters or their receptors causes the expected changes in activity. For example, acetylcholine at a neuromuscular junction produces muscle spasm or tetany. A large number of drugs are designed to alter the transmitter balance in some part of the body.

The data about receptors, transmitter activity and drugs form the basis for the theory that signals are carried from one neuron to another by a chemical transmitter. The theory was advanced early in this century, and the first experimental evidence supporting it came from the work of a German neurophysiologist, Otto Loewi, in 1921. Indeed, it is almost impossible to understand the nervous system without the transmitter theory, though it remains a theory until the receptors and the biochemical effects of the transmitter–receptor combination are described in detail.

In the brain, acetylcholine, dopamine and serotonin are excitatory. Noradrenaline is excitatory in some parts of the brain and inhibitory in others. GABA and glycine are inhibitory. In part of the mid-brain, glutamic acid excites and GABA inhibits signalling.

In the peripheral nervous system, the neurons outside the brain and spinal cord, the situation is both simpler and more confused. Simpler in that there are probably only two transmitters, acetylcholine and noradrenaline. More confused in that noradrenaline appears to be both excitatory and inhibitory, as it may be in the brain, but acetylcholine also may affect two classes of receptors each of which produces its own effects.

The peripheral nervous system is divided physiologically into the voluntary system which controls voluntary muscles in response to conscious commands, and the involuntary or autonomic nervous system, usually though not always beyond conscious control. In addition to their different roles, the two systems differ anatomically; for example, voluntary nerves run directly from the brain and spinal cord to the muscles they control whereas most involuntary nerves begin in ganglia outside the brain and spinal cord. Note, incidentally, that nerves consist of nerve cells, neurons. Nerves are often visible to the naked eye as thin white threads, but neurons cannot be seen without a microscope.

The autonomic nervous system itself has been traditionally subdivided into the sympathetic and the parasympathetic. An organ such as the walls of the intestine is regulated by nerves from both divisions. Where one division increases the activity of the organ, the other decreases it. For example, the sympathetic inhibits contractions of the intestinal wall whereas the parasympathetic excites contractions. In general, the sympathetic is active in times of stress. The parasympathetic functions are less clearly defined, being much more diffuse, but by speeding up food movement through the intestines and assisting defecation and micturition, the parasympathetic tends to empty the body.

There are also anatomical differences between the sympathetic and parasympathetic arising out of their different origins in the central nervous system. All three systems – voluntary, sympathetic and parasympathetic – consist of two sets of neurons: those running from the central nervous system to the periphery carrying orders from the centre, and those running from sensory organs to the central nervous system carrying information.

The voluntary nervous system and the parasympathetic division of the autonomic system are *cholinergic*, energized by acetylcholine. The sympathetic is *adrenergic*, energized by noradrenaline. Note that there are no inhibitory transmitters in the peripheral nervous system. In the parasympathetic, acetylcholine affects two classes of receptors identified as nicotinic and muscarinic because nicotine (the drug found in tobacco) affects one and another drug, muscarine, the other. Neither of these drugs occur naturally in the body (although, see *niacin*), but they have been used experimentally to clarify the different effects produced by acetylcholine. Muscarinic neurons occur in the eyes, lungs, heart, large arteries, salivary glands (see *saliva*) stomach, gut, bladder and some ganglia. Nicotinic receptors are found in most ganglia and also in voluntary muscles.

The two broad classes of noradrenergic receptors are designated alpha and beta. Like the nicotinic and muscarinic cholinergic receptors, the alpha and beta adrenergic receptors were defined by their different responses to drugs: in this case, to *adrenaline*, the *hormone* which is the breakdown product of noradrenaline, and to isoprenaline, an artificial substance. Alpha receptors respond more to adrenaline whereas beta receptors respond more to isoprenaline.

On the whole, alpha receptors are excitatory in the presence of noradrenaline, causing muscles to contract for example, and beta receptors are inhibitory. The most important exception to this general rule is in the heart where the response to noradrenaline is reversed: alpha receptors are inhibitory, and the beta receptors, excitatory. Thus, the stimulant effect of adrenaline injected directly into the heart arises because the drug molecules come into contact with beta receptors. The terminological confusion is sometimes overcome by labelling beta receptors in heart muscle, B1, and all other beta receptors, B2. It has also been suggested that the heart muscle beta receptors should be labelled, C. A further subdivision of alpha receptors into alpha 1 and alpha 2 has been introduced, moreover, the former being excitatory and the latter inhibitory (see also *noradrenaline*).

Because of the number of drugs that are designed to alter the behaviour of peripheral nerves, it is perhaps more useful to drop the traditional physiological and anatomical division of the peripheral nervous system in favour of classification by the transmitters involved. It is hardly surprising, furthermore, that these drugs display many undesirable side effects. Their activity is complicated by the refusal of the nervous system to allow simple classification and the tendency of most drugs, given the administrative techniques now used, to reach far beyond the affected tissues. Drugs meant to change the activities of transmitters in the brain may be even harder to control.

Triglyceride (see *Lipid*)

Trypsin

An *enzyme* secreted by the pancreas into the upper intestine where it splits *proteins*. Trypsin acts to break *peptide* bonds linking lysine or arginine to another *amino acid*. Trypsin also converts chymotrypsinogen to the enzyme, *chymotrypsin*.

It is formed in the pancreas as trypsinogen. Enzymes from the stomach digestive juices (see *pepsin*) or trypsin itself cause the precursor to split, releasing trypsin.

Tyrosine (see *Pepsin*)

Uracil

A *base* found in some *nucleotides* and *ribonucleic acid* (RNA). In *deoxyribonucleic acid*, uracil is replaced by another base, *thymine*. In RNA which contains a pairing of complementary bases, uracil is *hydrogen*-bonded to *adenine*.

Several nucleotides contain uracil. The most important is uridine-diphosphate glucose which acts as a *coenzyme* in the biological interconversion of *sugars*. Uracil is one of a class of compounds called pyrimidines with the structural formula:

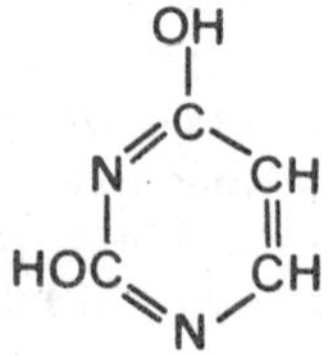

Urea

A waste product formed by the liver from the breakdown of *amino acids* which is excreted in the urine.

Urea was synthesized by the German chemist, Wöhler, in 1828, the first organic compound to be created artificially in a laboratory. It is also called carbamide. Its formula is: $CO(NH_2)_2$.

Urea is the principal method of excreting *nitrogen*. If the average intake of dietary *protein* contains 16 per cent nitrogen, a daily diet containing 100 grams of protein yields 16 grams of nitrogen. Roughly 16 grams of nitrogen are excreted each day in the urine. The daily excretion of urea is 30 grams of which about 14 grams are nitrogen. The remaining two grams of nitrogen are got rid of in *sweat* and faeces.

The *blood* normally carries about 30 mg of urea per 100 ml. In kidney failure, blood urea rises causing uraemia. Urea itself is not toxic, but the imbalance in blood-borne *electrolytes* which accompanies uraemia can be rapidly fatal.

In the liver, urea is actually formed from ammonia, itself the breakdown product of amino acids. The process of urea formation is cyclic in a manner analogous to the *citric acid* cycle. Indeed, the urea cycle was first described by the German-born British biochemist, Hans Krebs, who also identified the citric acid cycle.

Uric acid

A waste product formed in cells throughout the body by the breakdown of purine *bases, adenine* and *guanine*, and from dietary purines such as caffeine. Uric acid may also be synthesized from the *amino acid, glycine*.

Uric acid was discovered in urine by the Swedish chemist, Scheele, in 1776. It differs from other organic *acids* because the molecule contains no carboxyl (COOH) group. Its most common structural formula is:

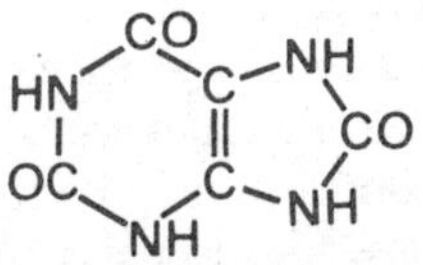

Normally, the *blood* contains about 3 mg of uric acid per ml. A gram a day is excreted in the urine. If the blood level of uric acid rises abnormally, uric acid *salts* (usually *sodium* mono-urate) may be deposited in the joints causing the pain

187

and swelling of gout. Drugs that treat the disease increase urinary clearance of uric acid.

In dogs excepting Dalmatians and in most other mammals, uric acid is converted to allantoin before excretion. No uric acid appears in the urine.

Urine (see *Renin, Urea, Uric acid*)

Vasopressin (Anti-diuretic hormone)

A *hormone* secreted by the posterior pituitary gland though it is probably formed by nerve cells in the hypothalamus, that portion of the mid-brain to which the pituitary is attached. Vasopressin may travel into the pituitary in nerve cells linking the gland to the hypothalamus. Its major function is to decrease the amount of water excreted in urine. Thus, it is an anti-diuretic because it reduces diuresis, the process of urine formation. In larger amounts, vasopressin raises blood pressure by causing capillary constriction.

It is secreted in response to an increase in the osmotic pressure of the *blood* caused by an increased blood concentration of *electrolytes*. Vasopressin hastens the return of water to the blood from the tissue fluid and by reabsorption through kidney tubules to equalize the osmotic pressure. Less urine is excreted. The osmotic pressure of blood affects specially adapted sensory nerve cells called osmoreceptors in the hypothalamus. Either these cells or nearby nerve cells secrete vasopressin.

Emotions such as anger and fear are signalled by nerve cells in the hypothalamus, and they are also accompanied by increased output of vasopressin. In strong emotional stress, so much vasopressin may be released that the blood vessels in the skin are constricted, causing pallor. Fainting and exercise are also causes of vasopressin secretion, perhaps because in both cases there is a need to pool available blood to assure adequate supplies to the brain and muscles, respectively. Emotions, fainting and exercise are all accompanied by a temporary fall in urine excretion, too.

Normally, vasopressin output is diurnal, increasing at night and thus contributing to the nocturnal decline in urine formation.

Vasopressin may also play a role in body temperature regulation, another function of nerve cells in the hypothalamus. To perform this role, vasopressin may be acting as a *transmitter* of signals between nerve cells and not as a hormone.

Vasopressin output has been associated with improved memory in experimental animals. It is not yet known whether this interesting effect is caused by some direct action of vasopressin on brain cells, for example in midbrain regions near the hypothalamus, or by the increased alertness resulting from the constriction of blood vessels and increased blood pressure produced by the hormone.

A tumour or some other disease affecting the hypothalamus can cause a failure of vasopressin secretion. The patient may then experience an enormous increase in urine formation accompanied by intense thirst. This condition is known as diabetes insipidus. It can be treated with injected vasopressin.

Vasopressin increases the reabsorption of water which has already been filtered out of the blood into the kidney tubules (see *renin*). The hormone appears to bind to a specific *receptor* in kidney tubule cell membranes causing formation of *cyclic adenosine monophosphate* (cAMP). Cyclic AMP in turn activates a sequence of poorly understood events leading to increased permeability of the tubule cell membranes.

Vasopressin is a *peptide* consisting of nine *amino acids*. Its structure is very similar to that of *oxytocin* (and is shown in that entry), also a posterior pituitary hormone.

Visual pigment (see *Iodopsin*)

Vitamin

A nutrient required in minute quantities to maintain life. The word vitamin, literally amine of life, was created by the

German chemist, Funk, because *thiamine*, the first vitamin to be identified, contains *nitrogen*. Most vitamins are not amines. All are essential because they participate in a vital chemical process without which life cannot continue. Non-human animals, bacteria and many plants can synthesize some if not all vitamins.

The discovery of vitamins has been of the greatest importance in the elimination of deficiency diseases such as pellagra (see *niacin*), scurvy (*ascorbic acid*) and pernicious anaemia (see *cyanocobalamin*). By and large, the average British and American diets contain adequate vitamin content, but there are exceptions. For example, the children of some working mothers, so-called 'latch-key' children, may subsist on a diet of chips and sweets which gives them ample energy supplies (see *carbohydrate, fat*), but is poor in vitamin A, the B vitamins and vitamin C. These children may display signs of deficiency diseases.

Immigrants to Britain who were born in India or Pakistan, and who suffer severely from vitamin-D deficiency are even more striking examples. Vitamin D is the sunshine vitamin. Indian children of immigrant parents may develop rickets, and the adults, osteomalacia, the equivalent *bone* disorder. Their traditional diets are low in fish oils containing vitamin D, but they have always obtained most of their vitamin D from sunlight which causes its biosynthesis in skin cells. In the northern British climate, without the hot semi-tropical sun, vitamin-D deficiency is a real threat.

It is possible to eat too much of some vitamins with serious effects. The B vitamins and vitamin C are water soluble and any excess is quickly excreted in the urine. Vitamins A, D, E and K, on the other hand, are *fat* soluble. Excesses are taken up by fat cells and can be broken down and excreted only very slowly. Though it is rare, an overdose of a fat-soluble vitamin does happen. There are people, for example, who try to subsist on a freak faddish diet such as carrot juice which is rich in vitamin A. Vitamin A in excess causes softening of the nails and hardening of the skin followed by severe nervous disorders and death. It is important to exercise care when taking vitamin-containing compounds and with specialized diets. The

Vitamin	Constituent of:	Functions	Deficiency disorders	Dietary sources
A	Retinene (see *Iodopsin*)	Visual pigments; normal growth, skin and hard tissues (hair, nails)	Night blindness, dermatitis, nervous disorders, widespread infections	Carrots, green veg, fish liver oils
Biotin (a B vitamin)	Carboxylases, a co-enzyme	Normal energy formation and storage	Nervous disorders, baldness, weakness, *acid–base* imbalances (rare except possibly in infants)	Most foods. Intestinal bacteria. Deficiency may be due to excess egg white, inherited disorder, bowel surgery
D (Calciferol)	None known	*Calcium* and *potassium* absorption and use, in concert with calcitonin and *parathormone*	Rickets, osteomalacia, infantile tetany	Fish liver oils; sunshine
E (Tocopherol)	Chemically similar to enzyme (see function)	Correct synthesis of *porphyrin* and *haemoglobin*	Vitamin-E anaemia	Wheat-germ oil
K (Phytonadione, Menadione)	Unknown	Correct synthesis of *blood factors* (VII, IX, X and prothrombin), carbohydrate interconversion	Increased bleeding, weakness	Various foods. Intestinal bacteria supply K for absorption

wisest course is probably always to consult a doctor before embarking on any therapy.

Ascorbic acid, cyanocobalamin (vitamin B_{12}), *folic acid*, niacin (vitamin B_3), *pyridoxine* (vitamin B_6), *riboflavin* (vitamin B_2) and thiamine (vitamin B_1) have been described. The table on p. 191 lists the remaining vitamins, the *coenzymes* or other compound of which they form a part, their physiological or biochemical function, the deficiency diseases that occur in their absence and the best dietary sources.

Vitreous humour

The high-viscosity fluid which fills the larger part of the eyeball behind the lens.

The viscosity is due to the presence of *hyaluronic acid* and *protein*. The aqueous humour in the space in front of the lens is more watery because it contains no hyaluronic acid. Both humours are formed from *lymph* by cells in the wall of the eyeball.

Appendix 1
Hydrocarbons and Amines

The formulae for *carbohydrates*, fatty acids (see *lipid*) and *sugars* are consistent and may be generalized for all members of the respective categories. Thus, all fatty acids are $CH_3(CH_2)_nCOOH$, where n is an even number.

Many other organic compounds build up in an analogous way with generalizable formulae. For example, the saturated hydrocarbons (those with only single covalent bonds; see Appendix 3) have the general formula: $C_nH_{2n}+2$. These hydrocarbons also give their names to prefixes widely used in compounds containing the correct number of carbon atoms or the hydrocarbon itself as a group at one end of the molecule. Unsaturated hydrocarbons (lacking one H) are alkyl groups or radicals which cannot exist independently of other groups.

Saturated hydrocarbon	Formula	Prefix	Unsaturated hydrocarbon	Formula
Methane	CH_4	meth-	methyl	CH_3-
Ethane	C_2H_6	eth-	ethyl	C_2H_5-
Propane	C_3H_8	prop-	propyl	C_3H_7-
Butane	C_4H_{10}	but-	butyl	C_4H_9
Pentane	C_5H_{12}	pent-		but
Hexane	C_6H_{14}	hex-	propyl = $CH_3CH_2CH_2-$	
Heptane	C_7H_{16}	hept-	isopropyl = $CH_3CH^{\circ}CH_3-$	
Octane	C_8H_{18}	oct-	and so on with	
and so on			greater complexity	

Similarly, there are suffixes in the names of compounds which indicate the atoms or groups of atoms at the end of the molecule which confer on it a characteristic function; for example, COOH, a carboxyl, is an *acid*. Others used in this book are:

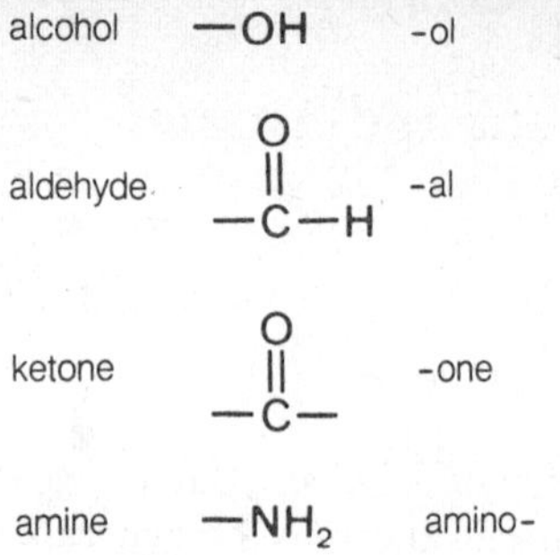

alcohol   —OH   -ol

aldehyde

$$-\overset{\displaystyle O}{\underset{\displaystyle }{\overset{\displaystyle \|}{C}}}-H$$

-al

ketone

$$-\overset{\displaystyle O}{\underset{\displaystyle }{\overset{\displaystyle \|}{C}}}-$$

-one

amine   —NH$_2$ amino-

The amines are all derived from ammonia (NH$_3$) by the substitution of alkyl groups for one, two or all three of the hydrogen atoms. As a result, there are primary, secondary and tertiary amines, respectively. The *amino acids* contain primary amines (NH$_2$) plus a carboxyl group.

The *peptide* bond is also called an amide bond.

The saturated hydrocarbons described above are all straight-line chains of carbon atoms:

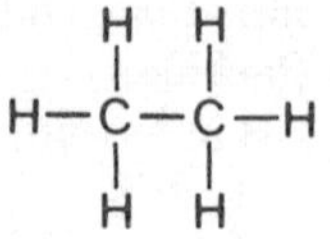

$$H-\overset{H}{\underset{H}{C}}-\overset{H}{\underset{H}{C}}-H \qquad\qquad H-\overset{H}{\underset{H}{C}}-\overset{H}{\underset{H}{C}}-\overset{H}{\underset{H}{C}}-\overset{H}{\underset{H}{C}}-H$$

C_2H_6 = ethane 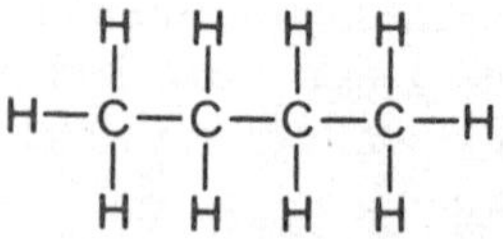 C_4H_{10} = butane

These are called aliphatic compounds. Hydrocarbons may also take up ring formations which are always unsaturated. The most familiar is benzene (C$_6$H$_6$):

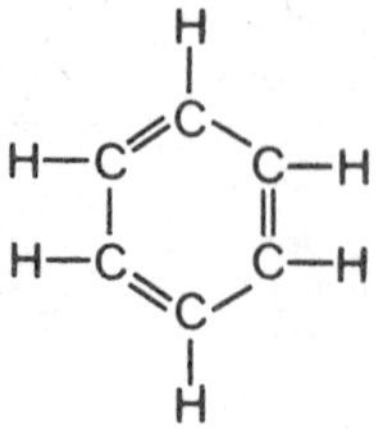

This representation of the double bonds as fixed between the three pairs of atoms forming the ring is highly stylized and physically unlikely. The doubling of bonding reflects valency changes (see Appendix 3) due to electron movement and probably shifts back and forth amongst all six-carbon atoms forming the ring. It is sometimes drawn

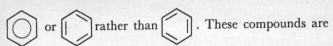 . These compounds are

called aromatic because all of them were thought to have a smell, like benzene does. All sugars, *catecholamines* and *steroids* and many fatty acids and local *hormones* are ring-based molecules.

Appendix 2
pH, Equivalents and Constants

It is often desirable to measure the acidity or alkalinity of a solution, especially of *body fluids*. pH (the H stands for *hydrogen*) is a scale in terms of which such a measurement can be made.

The acidity of a solution is due to the concentration of hydrogen *ions* and not the concentration of the parent molecule. For example, *hydrochloric acid* is a strong *acid* and *carbonic acid*, weak, because of the relative numbers of H^+ released by each acid.

Water consists of a hydrogen atom bound to a hydroxyl (OH) group. Pure water is incapable of conducting an electrical current because it contains very few ions. Even in pure water, however, a small number of water molecules are ionized to H^+ and OH^-. These ionized molecules can be counted and have been found to equal 10^{-7} mole per litre. A mole is the basic unit of measurement of the amount of a substance. The standard unit is the number of atoms in 12 grams of carbon (see Appendix 3, atomic weight). The substance to be measured may be atoms, molecules, ions, electrons or any other portion of matter. Thus, a mole of H^+ is the number of ions of hydrogen, and 10^{-7} is the negative logarithm – a very small number indeed.

Now let us resort to a few simple formulae:

(1) $[H^+] [OH^-] = K$

where the brackets signify ion concentration (that is, moles per litre) and K = concentration. Then

(2) $[H^+ = 10^{-7}] [OH^- = 10^{-7}] = 10^{-14}$

Formula (2) states the situation with pure water. Any variation in H^+ concentration will be balanced by the opposite variation in concentration of OH^-. By adding an acid, the H^+ concentration is increased to, let us say, $[H^+ = 10^{-1}]$.

(3) $[10^{-1}] [OH^-] = 10^{-14}$
$[OH^-] = 10^{-13}$

At the same time, in other words, OH^- declines to $[OH^- = 10^{-13}]$.

pH is the negative logarithm of concentration stated as a positive number. Thus, a neutral pH is 7:

(4) $pH = -\log [10^{-7}] = -(-7) = 7$

The acidic solution in formula (3) has a pH of 1. Any pH below 7 is acid, but pH 1 is a much more acid solution than pH 5. Conversely, pH over 7 is basic or alkaline, and the higher the pH (13.999 . . . being the maximum) the more basic the solution.

Using a related standard of measurement (mmol/l of charges = millimole per litre of charges), it is possible to show the positive and negative ions in the body fluids when they are in acid–base balance.

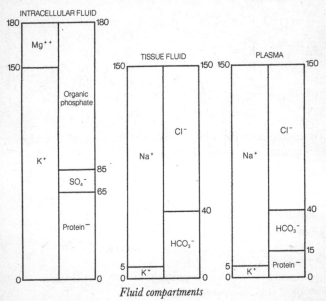

Fluid compartments

The bar graph for intracellular fluids is taller than those for the other two fluid compartments because the cell contains more ions per litre.

The following equivalents and constants may also be useful:

1 calorie (c) = the amount of heat required to raise the temperature of 1 gm of water from 14 degrees to 15 degrees Centigrade.

1 Calorie (C) = 1000 calories

1 Calorie = 4185.5 joules = 4.186 k joules

1 joule (J) = the energy produced by 1 watt of electricity in 1 second. The joule is the new S.I. (*Système International d'Unités*) unit of force.

Temperature

F = Fahrenheit
C = Centigrade or Celsius
K = Kelvin, the SI unit of temperature

0 degrees	K =	−273.15	degrees	C =	−459.67	degrees	F
233	K =	−40		C =	−40		F
273	K =	0		C =	32		F
283	K =	10		C =	50		F
310	K =	37		C =	98.6		F
313	K =	40		C =	104		F
373	K =	100		C =	212		F

To interconvert C and F, take one of the equivalents, above, and multiply or divide degrees above or below by 1.8.

45 degrees C = [5 × 1.8 = 9.0] + 104 = 113 degrees F

Mass

1 gram (gm)	=	.03527 oz (avoir.)
1 kilogram (kg)	=	2.20462 lbs
1 lb	=	.4536 kg
1 oz	=	28.350 gm

Volume

1 litre (l)	=	61.0239 inches^3 (in)^3
	=	1.76 pints
	=	.22 gallons (gal)
1 pint (UK)	=	.568 l
(US)	=	.4544 l
1 gallon (UK)	=	4.546 l
(US)	=	3.651 l

Length

1 metre (m)	=	39.370113 inches (in)
	=	3.2808 feet (ft)
	=	1.0936 yards (yd)
1 inch	=	2.54 centimetres (cm) exactly
1 foot	=	30.48 cm exactly
1 yard	=	.9144 m exactly
1 mile	=	1.6093 kilometres (km)

Appendix 3
Elements and Bonds

In the 1850s, the Russian chemist, D. I. Mendeleev, arranged the elements in a table based on the weights of their atoms and divided into groups of 7 or 8. The corresponding members of each group show relationships in chemical properties; elements with characteristics that are similar recur at regular intervals throughout the series. Mendeleev was able to use his periodic table, based on the periodic law, to predict that certain elements would be found where blanks then appeared in the table. The first three were gallium (1871), scandium (1879) and germanium (1886). Mendeleevium, atomic number 101, was discovered in the debris from an atomic explosion in 1952.

Atomic number = the number of protons in the nucleus of an atom. In the neutral atom, these protons are electrically balanced by an equal number of electrons outside the nucleus

Atomic weight = relative atomic mass calculated in relation to the mass of a carbon atom (see also Appendix 2, pH)

Molecular weight = the sum of the atomic weights of all the atoms in a molecule

Periodic table of the elements

1A	2A	3B	4B	5B	6B	7B	8			1B	2B	3A	4A	5A	6A	7A	0
1 H																	2 He
3 Li	4 Be											5 B	6 C	7 N	8 O	9 F	10 Ne
11 Na	12 Mg											13 Al	14 Si	15 P	16 S	17 Cl	18 Ar
19 K	20 Ca	21 Sc	22 Ti	23 V	24 Cr	25 Mn	26 Fe	27 Co	28 Ni	29 Cu	30 Zn	31 Ga	32 Ge	33 As	34 Se	35 Br	36 Kr
37 Rb	38 Sr	39 Y	40 Zr	41 Nb	42 Mo	43 Tc	44 Ru	45 Rh	46 Pd	47 Ag	48 Cd	49 In	50 Sn	51 Sb	52 Te	53 I	54 Xe
55 Cs	56 Ba	57* La	72 Hf	73 Ta	74 W	75 Re	76 Os	77 Ir	78 Pt	79 Au	80 Hg	81 Tl	82 Pb	83 Bi	84 Po	85 At	86 Rn
87 Fr	88 Ra	89† Ac															

TRANSITION ELEMENTS (3B → 2B)

*Lanthanides		57 La	58 Ce	59 Pr	60 Nd	61 Pm	62 Sm	63 Eu	64 Gd	65 Tb	66 Dy	67 Ho	68 Er	69 Tm	70 Yb	71 Lu	
†Actinides		89 Ac	90 Th	91 Pa	92 U	93 Np	94 Pu	95 Am	96 Cm	97 Bk	98 Cf	99 Es	100 Fm	101 Md	102 No	103 Lr	

Elements and Bonds

The Elements arranged in Alphabetical Order of their Chemical Symbol

Symbol	Name	Atomic Number	Atomic Weight	Symbol	Name	Atomic Number	Atomic Weight
A or Ar	Argon	18	39.944	Mn	Manganese	25	54.94
Ac	Actinium	89	227	Mo	Molybdenum	42	95.95
Ag	Silver	47	107.880	N	Nitrogen	7	14.008
Al	Aluminium	13	26.98	Na	Sodium	11	22.991
Am	Americium	95	(243)	Nb	Niobium	41	92.91
As	Arsenic	33	74.91	Nd	Neodymium	60	144.27
At	Astatine	85	(210)	Ne	Neon	10	20.183
Au	Gold	79	197.0	Ni	Nickel	28	58.71
B	Boron	5	10.82	Np	Neptunium	93	(237)
Ba	Barium	56	137.36	O	Oxygen	8	16
Be	Beryllium	4	9.013	Os	Osmium	76	190.2
Bi	Bismuth	83	209.00	P	Phosphorus	15	30.975
Bk	Berkelium	97	(249)*	Pa	Protoactinium	91	(231)
Br	Bromine	35	79.916	Pb	Lead	82	207.21
C	Carbon	6	12.011	Pd	Palladium	46	106.4
Ca	Calcium	20	40.08	Pm	Promethium	61	(147)*
Cd	Cadmium	48	112.41	Po	Polonium	84	(210)*
Ce	Cerium	58	140.13	Pr	Praseodymium	59	140.92
Cf	Californium	98	(251)*	Pt	Platinum	78	195.09
Cl	Chlorine	17	35.457	Pu	Plutonium	94	(242)
Cm	Curium	96	(247)	Ra	Radium	88	(226)
Co	Cobalt	27	58.94	Rb	Rubidium	37	85.48
Cr	Chromium	24	52.01	Re	Rhenium	75	186.22
Cs	Caesium	55	132.91	Rh	Rhodium	45	102.91
Cu	Copper	29	63.54	Rn	Radon	86	(222)
Dy	Dysprosium	66	162.51	Ru	Ruthenium	44	101.1
Er	Erbium	68	167.27	S	Sulphur	16	32.066 ±0.003
Es	Einsteinium	99	(254)				
Eu	Europium	63	152.0	Sb	Antimony	51	121.76
F	Fluorine	9	19.00	Sc	Scandium	21	44.96
Fe	Iron	26	55.85	Se	Selenium	34	78.96
Fm	Fermium	100	(253)	Si	Silicon	14	28.09
Fr	Francium	87	(223)	Sm	Samarium	62	150.35
Ga	Gallium	31	69.72	Sn	Tin	50	118.70
Gd	Gadolinium	64	157.26	Sr	Strontium	38	87.63
Ge	Germanium	32	72.60	Ta	Tantalum	73	180.95
H	Hydrogen	1	1.0080	Tb	Terbium	65	158.93
He	Helium	2	4.003	Tc	Technetium	43	(99)*
Hf	Hafnium	72	178.50	Te	Tellurium	52	127.61
Hg	Mercury	80	200.61	Th	Thorium	90	232.05
Ho	Holmium	67	164.94	Ti	Titanium	22	47.90
I	Iodine	53	126.91	Tl	Thallium	81	204.39
In	Indium	49	114.82	Tm	Thulium	69	168.94
Ir	Iridium	77	192.2	U	Uranium	92	238.07
K	Potassium	19	39.100	V	Vanadium	23	50.95
Kr	Krypton	36	83.80	W	Tungsten	74	183.86
La	Lanthanum	57	138.92	Xe	Xenon	54	131.30
Li	Lithium	3	6.940	Y	Yttrium	39	88.92
Lu	Lutetium	71	174.99	Yb	Ytterbium	70	173.04
Md	Mendeleevium	101	(256)	Zn	Zinc	30	65.38
Mg	Magnesium	12	24.32	Zr	Zirconium	40	91.22

Notes to the Alphabetical Table
The values given normally indicate the mean atomic weight of the mixture of isotopes found in nature. Particular attention is drawn to the value for sulphur, where the deviation shown is due to variation in relative concentration of isotopes.

Bracketed values refer to the individual isotopes of radioactive elements. In most cases the value for the most long lived is given. Where, however, an asterisk occurs the Atomic Weight is that of the better known isotope.

Bonds. A bond is the link established between atoms. It is formed by electrical attractive forces arising out of the presence or absence of electrons rotating around the nuclei of the respective atoms. A bond exists between only two atoms, but either of these two may also form a bond with a third, fourth or more atoms depending on the nature of the respective elements.

Thus, the first hydrocarbon, methane, is a carbon bound to four hydrogen atoms:

$$
\begin{array}{c}
\text{H} \\
| \\
\text{H} - \text{C} - \text{H} \\
| \\
\text{H}
\end{array}
$$

The bonds holding the carbon atom to each of the four hydrogens in methane are covalent. They are formed because the single hydrogen electron becomes at the same time a part of the carbon atom. From the standpoint of the carbon atom, the four hydrogen electrons complete the orbitals in the outer Principal Shell of electrons. Put differently, they increase the thermodynamic stability of the structure of the atom. Covalent bonds are the strongest that can be formed between atoms.

Ionic bonds are a special category of bonds analogous to covalent bonds in that the elements forming a molecule share electrons. Compounds formed by ionic bonds differ in that the elements are electrolytes. When the compound is dissolved in water, the elements are ionized. Ionic bonds occur in compounds that conduct electric currents. For example, NaCl is formed by ionic bonding and breaks down in water to form Na^+ and Cl^-. Water itself is an ionic compound, existing in part as H^+ and OH^-.

Several weaker types of bonds may be formed due to electromagnetic attractions between atoms which do not involve the exchange of electrons. In biology, the most important of these is the hydrogen bond (see, for example, *deoxyribonucleic acid, enzyme*). In a hydrogen bond, the link is always between hydrogen and another element, usually oxygen. In structural formulae, hydrogen bonds are often represented thus: $-H \ldots O-$.

Reference

A Dictionary of Mythologies   £1.95 ☐
Max Shapiro and Rhoda Hendricks
The first concise yet comprehensive dictionary of world mythologies. It is fully cross-referenced, so that the universal themes in common to all myths are easily recognized, and the cultural differences easily compared.

Test Your Own Wordpower   95p ☐
Hunter Diack
Test your own vocabulary by attempting these carefully devised tests. Shakespeare's was over 35,000 and the national average around 12,000.

The Encyclopaedia of Reality   £2.25 ☐
Katinka Matson
An indispensable reference book of alternative thought and of the ideas of the key revolutionary thinkers of the past and modern times.

Reference

The Englishman's Flora
£1.95 ☐
Geoffrey Grigson
A latter-day herbal of the medicinal and culinary purposes of the flowers and plants of the English countryside: magic, myth, lore and truth. Illustrated.

A Dictionary of Operations
£2.50 ☐
Dr Andrew Stanway
A lucid commonsense guide to hospitals and how they affect the patient plus an A-Z of operations and an alphabetical list of procedures and investigations.

The Oxford Companion to Ships and the Sea
£4.95 ☐
Edited by Peter Kemp
The complete guide to all things nautical. This compedium, with its lavish illustrations, is a wide-ranging survey of mariners, navigators, waterways, naval battles, knots, ocean theory and all the lore and customs of the sea.

A Dictionary of Symbols
£2.95 ☐
Tom Chetwynd
Tom Chetwynd has drawn from the collective wisdom of the great psychologists, particularly Jung, to create a comprehensive and thought-provoking guide to the language of symbols.

Halliwell's Film Guide
£3.95 ☐
Leslie Halliwell
A mammoth new Guide covering fifty years of English-language talkies and 8,000 films.

Halliwell's Teleguide
£2.95 ☐
Leslie Halliwell
An alphabetical Enquire Within Upon Television which will have appeal for everyone who has ever switched on a set.

Trees and Bushes of Britain and Europe
£2.95 ☐
Oleg Polunin
A superb and definitive guide. Fully illustrated in colour and carefully organized for use in the field.

Reference

How Things Work   £3.25 each ☐
Vols 1 & 2   or £5.95 set ☐
The Universal Encyclopedia of Machines. More than a reference
work, more than a browser's delight. *How Things Work* is an
essential resource and an accumulative answer to the whole
question of what makes the world go round. Each volume contains
over 1,000 illustrations.

A Dictionary of Drugs (New Edit)   £2.50 ☐
Richard B Fisher and George A Christie
From everyday aspirins and vitamins, to the powerful agents
prescribed for heart disease and cancer, this is a revised reference
guide to the gamut of drugs in today's pharmaceutical armoury.

A Dictionary of Symptoms   £2.95 ☐
Dr Joan Gomez
A thorough-going and authoritative guide to the interpretation of
symptoms of human disease.

Dictionary for Dreamers   £1.95 ☐
Tom Chetwynd
A comprehensive key to the baffling language of dream symbolism.
Over 500 archetypal symbols give essential clues to understanding
the ingeniously disguised, life-enriching, often urgent messages to
be found in dreams.

A Dictionary of Mental Health   £1.95 ☐
Richard B Fisher
A useful, sensible guide around the confusing world of mental
health, mental illness and its treatment.

Body Magic, An Encyclopaedia of Esoteric Man   £2.25 ☐
Benjamin Walker
This is a guide to the occult significances of the human body.
Arranged alphabetically it deals with separate anatomical and
physiological items, functions, psychology, parapsychology,
mystical and magical concepts of the body.

All these books are available at your local bookshop or newsagent, and can be ordered direct from the publisher or from Dial-A-Book Service.

To order direct from the publisher just tick the titles you want and fill in the form below:

Name _____

Address _____

_____

Send to:
Granada Cash Sales
PO Box 11, Falmouth, Cornwall TR10 9EN

Please enclose remittance to the value of the cover price plus:

UK 45p for the first book, 20p for the second book plus 14p per copy for each additional book ordered to a maximum charge of £1.63.

BFPO and Eire 45p for the first book, 20p for the second book plus 14p per copy for the next 7 books, thereafter 8p per book.

Overseas 75p for the first book and 21p for each additional book.

To order from Dial-A-Book Service, 24 hours a day, 7 days a week:

Telephone 01 836 2641 – give name, address, credit card number and title required. The books will be sent to you by post.

DIAL·A·BOOK

Granada Publishing reserve the right to show new retail prices on covers, which may differ from those previously advertised in the text or elsewhere.